Contents

D0470198

SPEECH COMMUNICATION FOR INTERNATIONAL STUDENTS

PAULETTE DALE • *JAMES C. WOLF*

Miami-Dade Community College

 Prentice Hall Regents, Englewood Cliffs, NJ 07632

Library of Congress Cataloging-in-Publication Data

DALE, PAULETTE.
   Speech communication for international students.

   1. Public speaking.   2. English language—Textbooks
for foreign speakers.   I. Wolf, James C., 1946–
II. Title.
PN4121.D324   1988   808.5'1   87-25889
ISBN 0-13-827312-X

Editorial/production supervision
and interior design: Virginia Rubens
Manufacturing buyer: Margaret Rizzi

 © 1988 by Prentice Hall Regents
Prentice-Hall, Inc.
A Paramount Communications Company
Englewood Cliffs, New Jersey 07632

Printed in the United States of America

20 19 18 17 16

ISBN 0-13-827312-X

Prentice-Hall International (UK) Limited, *London*
Prentice-Hall of Australia Pty. Limited, *Sydney*
Prentice-Hall Canada Inc., *Toronto*
Prentice-Hall Hispanoamericana, S.A., *Mexico*
Prentice-Hall of India Private Limited, *New Delhi*
Prentice-Hall of Japan, Inc., *Tokyo*
Simon & Schuster Asia Pte. Ltd., *Singapore*
Editora Prentice-Hall do Brasil, Ltda., *Rio de Janeiro*

Preface

For more than thirty collective years the authors have been teaching speech communication classes composed largely of non-native speakers of English. We find that most of the available speech communication/public speaking texts written for American students are not appropriate for use with international students and do not meet their particular speech communication needs. Speech communication teachers of ESL/EFL students are not interested in discussing complicated communication theory and fancy terminology (communication dyads, triads, message channels, transmitters, etc.). Additionally, the examples and activities these books contain are not relevant to the backgrounds and experiences of international students. On the other hand, there is a variety of speech texts available written by those in the field of ESL/EFL. However, although called "speech," they are little more than advanced English conversation texts and are more appropriate for use in advanced conversation courses.

Our book, *Speech Communication for International Students*, is designed to meet the needs of advanced-level ESL/EFL students and their teachers. It recognizes that the primary goals of such a course are to help students to:

1. **develop confidence when expressing themselves before a group**

2. **reason logically**

3. **orally present their information, ideas, and opinions in a coherent, organized fashion**

4. **learn the basics of outlining and organizing a speech**

5. **learn the basics of informative and persuasive speaking**

6. **listen critically and objectively**

Most chapters are similar to those traditionally found in speech communication texts written for native speakers. A glance at the table of contents will reveal specific chapter titles and what they include. Chapters on "Listening" and "Understanding and Using Common Expressions" have been purposefully included in this book. The "Listening" chapter includes theory and practical activities designed to enhance English vocabulary and the ability to recognize important associations and relationships between concepts presented auditorily. The chapter on "Understanding and Using Common Expressions" is based on our belief that to communicate effectively in English, non-native speakers must be familiar with idiomatic expressions. This chapter is not intended to be an in-depth, definitive study of the area; however, our hope is that the result will be useful to international students of Speech Communication who wish to improve their ability to communicate naturally and informally in English. Of course, understanding idioms and appropriate expressions also enhances listening comprehension.

Most experts agree that a "learning by doing" approach is the best way to learn these or any skills. For this reason, there is a variety of mini-tests, review tests, and activities (listening exercises, outlining and information-organizing fun "tests," idiomatic expression and comprehension tasks, etc.) throughout the text designed to help students measure their own progress and understanding of the material. Various assignments encourage out-of-class practice prior to the actual presentation of an in-class assignment or speech.

An Instructor's Manual to accompany the text is available upon request from the publisher. It is a unique and vital reference tool for the instructor. It follows the book chapter by chapter and provides supplementary information to enhance the explanation of specific assignments, as well as a variety of hints about assigning, critiquing, and grading students' speech assignments. Teacher evaluation forms are provided and suggest what should be evaluated for each particular speech presentation.

Speech Communication for International Students will guide ESL/EFL students through the practical principles of speech communication while providing them with ideas for communication experiences which will enhance their vocabularies and knowledge of English form, structure, and use. Examples and explanations frequently refer to people from different ethnic and cultural backgrounds. Assignments and activities are of the same nature that students will face in real situations long after taking a speech course.

Acknowledgments

The authors wish to express their sincerest gratitude to the many people who assisted in developing this book:

Professor Tommie Ems of The College of Lake County; Professors Edward A. Anderson and Robert L. Levin of Miami Dade Community College; and our colleagues who recommended valuable improvements;

The following reviewers, who read the material and provided valuable feedback and suggestions for improvement: Kim Cox Carleton, Cristin Carpenter, Mary Ann Christison, Consuelo E. Stebbins, Marilyn VanHare, and Terry Wiley.

Our students, past, present, and future, for encouraging us and for giving us many practical suggestions to help us better meet their needs;

And our families for their support and encouragement throughout.

Introduction

Whether you are from Miami or New York, New Delhi or Tokyo, Taiwan or Mexico City, you will find the study of speech communication to be one of the most exciting, challenging, and positive learning experiences you may ever have.

The study of speech communication will engage you in one of the oldest academic subjects known. "Rhetoric," as the ancient Greeks called it, shares this distinction with philosophy and mathematics. So by studying speech communication, you are participating in an area that men and women for over two thousand years have thought to be essential to the functioning of a democratic state and to the individual within society.

The study of speech communication will help you improve your knowledge, attitudes, and skills. It will also help you grow in self-confidence, human understanding, listening skills, critical thinking, organization of your thoughts, the use of body and voice to communicate, and the ability to give and accept constructive criticism.

Throughout your life, you will give many types of speeches. You will need to be able to organize your thoughts logically, have self-confidence, and persuade others to your way of thinking. Success in many careers depends on good speech communication skills. These include careers in administration, government, public relations, personnel, politics, education, sales, and private industry. As you can see, the study of speech communication will be applicable to your lifetime needs.

The more effort you put into the study of speech communication, the more you will benefit. Of course, you are probably nervous about the idea of standing before an audience and making a speech. This fear is perfectly natural. Your fears will fade as you progress through this class. By the end of the semester, you will be proud of the progress you have made.

You will have many chances to speak in this class. Some of your speaking assignments will be ungraded. These will give you confidence and help you to improve other speeches. Your teacher will help you learn how to select topics and how to make them interesting to your audience. Think of your teacher as a friend who is there to help you over the problem spots and bring you successfully through the study of speech communication.

Daniel Webster, a famous American orator, once said,

> *"If all my talents and powers were to be taken from me by some inscrutable Providence, and I had my choice of keeping but one, I would unhesitatingly ask to be allowed to keep the Power of Speaking, for through it, I would quickly recover all the rest."*

Good luck and let's begin!

Speaking to Develop Self-Confidence

It is the beginning of the semester and this speech class has just begun. It is natural to be nervous about speaking in front of people you've never met before. *Relax*—your classmates will soon become new friends and will no longer seem like strangers.

This chapter is full of suggestions for presentations which will help you. Believe it or not, you are already prepared to deliver many excellent speeches. Talking about yourself, your personal experiences, opinions, and concerns or fears is the best way to do this. Your teacher will assign or ask you to choose from some of the speaking activities in this section of the book.

Confidence Building Speech #1:

SPEECH TO INTRODUCE YOURSELF

The best way for people to get to know one another in a class like this is to share autobiographical information. Your first assignment will be to make a speech about yourself. Because you should be very natural and spontaneous as you speak, you will not be allowed to write your speech and read it to the class. We will describe two different methods for you to use when preparing and presenting your speech to introduce yourself.

METHOD #1

Try to think of your speech as if it were a photo album. As your eyes move from picture to picture, you recall different events and happenings in your life and interesting things about yourself. Pictures make it possible for you to talk in front of a group of people comfortably and naturally. You will find that by using simple pictures as your speaking "notes" you will never forget what you want to say. You will be able to talk through your speech with your audience in a relaxed manner needing only an occasional glance down at your pictures to trigger your memory.

Your assignment is to draw 4 or 5 different sets of pictures which will remind you what to say about yourself. You should draw a different picture for each piece of information you want to share with your audience. **Don't worry if you are not an artist!** The ability to draw is not important. What *is* important is that your pictures help you to remember to tell us about yourself (your background, family, interests, hobbies, future goals). Your teacher and classmates want to get to know you. Remember, "A picture is worth a thousand words." There is no need to write a speech on paper—your pictures will be your notes!

EXAMPLE 1: If you would like to tell the class that you come from Japan and live in a big house with your parents and three older brothers named Teruo, Kim, and Takahiko, you could draw:

EXAMPLE 2: If you would like to mention that you came to the United States two years ago and lived in New York for one year before moving to Miami, you could draw:

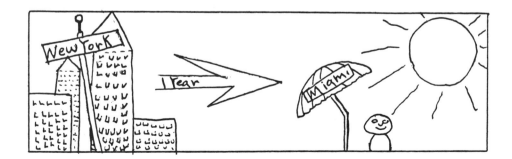

EXAMPLE 3: If you would like to talk about some of your hobbies which include listening to music, reading books, and going sailing and fishing, you could draw:

EXAMPLE 4: If you would like to tell us that you are studying photography and hope to be a famous underwater photographer some day, you could draw:

We suggest you draw each set of pictures on a separate piece of paper with a dark marking pen so they are easily seen by everyone. **You'll do great! Just use your imagination and be creative!**

METHOD #2

Read the following ten questions to yourself and answer them as completely as possible, with as many examples as you can think of. When it is your turn to make your speech, you may use the questions as a guide to help you organize your thoughts. It will not be necessary to write your speech on paper. A quick look at the questions while you are speaking will help remind you what to say about yourself.

1. **What is your name?** (Be sure to say your name clearly. If it is unusual, spell it for the class.)

2. **Where are you from and how long have you been in this country?**

3. **Why did you come to this country?**

4. **How many brothers or sisters do you have?** (Give names and ages.)

5. **Who do you live with?**

6. **What are you studying here?** (Describe the other classes you are taking.)

7. **What do you like to do in your free time?**

8. **What hobbies or special interests do you have?**

9. **What are some of your future plans and goals?**

10. **How do you think you will benefit from taking this course?**

These ten questions are meant to help guide you through your speech, not limit what you say. Try to think of other things which will help the class learn more about you. You are invited to tell us even *more* about yourself!

Now that you've had a chance to become acquainted with all your classmates, you probably feel more comfortable about the thought of speaking in front of them. As your teacher will soon ask you to make some of the other speeches in this chapter, it's time to think about the many different topics that you are already prepared to talk about.

Brainstorming for Speech Topics

Think of experiences you've had while growing up, different opinions and fears you have, and people, places, or objects that have played an important role in your life. Use the worksheet on page 7 and list as many possible speech topics as you can think of. *Be specific*. Your teacher will help you choose which topics will make for the most interesting classroom presentations. Below are some general examples of topics for your list. Be sure to think of at least ten more of your own.

My Opinion of This City	Serving in My Country's Military
Why I Like College	My Fear of Boats
An Embarrassing Moment	Learning to Fly a Plane
A Day I'll Always Remember	My Most Pleasant Memory
My First Date	My First Job
The Time I Ran Away from Home	

TOPICS I'M PREPARED TO SPEAK ABOUT

Personal Experiences I've Had

Opinions I Feel Strongly About

Fears/Concerns I Have

Activities I'm Good At

You probably feel more confident already knowing that you now have a variety of topics to talk about. Before making your first presentation, you should become familiar with some basic speech delivery techniques.

Suggestions for Delivering Your Speeches

Your speech is more than just the words you use. *How* you say something is just as important as *what* you say.

Good delivery involves several important aspects. To develop it, you must practice. Remember to be yourself—just speak the way you do in everyday conversation with your friends. The following basic techniques for delivering a speech will help you to improve your own individual style of public speaking.

1. ***Stage Fright:*** First, let's face one problem about speaking in public which concerns most beginning students—*nervousness*. Most people are nervous about public speaking. Ask your classmates! Even some teachers feel nervous when they meet a new class for the first time. The good news is that you can learn to control your nervousness rather than let it get you down.

Try to accept nervousness as a natural way of helping you to be alert and to do your best. You will be able to reduce your nervousness and, after a few speeches, you will understand and accept it. Remember, it is normal and natural for you to be a little nervous!

How will you be able to reduce this tension? Well, the best tip we can give you is to be really well prepared. If you know that your topic is interesting, and that your material is well organized, you have already reduced a major worry!

2. ***Have Good Posture:*** Posture is the way that you stand before your audience. Do not lean on a lectern. Try to stand naturally erect. If there is no lectern in the room, place yourself in a good visible position in the middle of the room. You should try to look casual—but not sloppy.

3. ***Facial Expression:*** If you smile before you start your speech you give your audience the impression that you are not nervous and are looking forward to speaking. Don't fake a big smile—just a small natural smile will do. During your speech try to change your facial expressions to convey the emotions that you feel. Throughout your speech you need to use expressive and animated facial expressions.

4. ***Movement and Gestures:*** Movement and gestures help your audience to understand the meaning of your speech. They also help you to express emotions connected with these meanings.

If you are nervous, take a few steps to your right or left while speaking. This will help you to relax and move naturally. Don't stand "frozen" in one place for your entire speech.

Gestures are your hand and arm movements. Gestures help you to relax. Gestures also help you to emphasize important points in your speech.

Always start your speech with your hands hanging naturally at your sides. Keep them down until you feel like emphasizing a point—then use your hands as you would in everyday conversation. The following types of gestures may help you to use your hands naturally.

a. *Make size clear:* You could show the width or height of an object by using your hands.

b. *Emphasize an idea:* You could pound on the lectern to show your anger about the Communist takeover in Cuba, for example.

c. *Symbolic action:* You could wave your hand in a friendly greeting gesture to show how you felt when you saw a long-lost friend.

d. *Show location:* You could indicate locations or directions by pointing your index finger. You could use your hand in a sweeping motion to show your audience how the 100 or so islands, islets, and cays that make up the U.S. Virgin Islands are clustered in the sparkling Caribbean sea.

5. **Eye Contact:** Eye contact customs vary from culture to culture. In some Eastern cultures women are expected to lower their eyes in communication situations. In other cultures it is a sign of respect to lower one's eyes when speaking to older people.

In some countries, however, it is the custom to look your audience straight in the eye. You should not look at the floor or out the window because this will give the audience the idea that you are not interested in your topic or in them. The idea is to *give the impression* that you are talking to each individual in your audience. If you have a large audience you can't actually look at each person's eyes, but you can casually move your eyes from one section of the audience to another throughout your speech. Try to look at people in the middle of the room, then slowly look to the right side of the room, then to the left side, then back to the center of the room.

You will find that if you look directly at your audience, their nods, gestures, and smiles will let you know that they understand you. This positive feedback will make you feel better and less nervous.

6. **Speak with Enthusiasm:** Enthusiasm is being lively and showing your own personal concern for your subject and your audience. Act as though you really care about your speech. Your voice should be strong;

you should *want* to communicate. If you are truly interested in your topic, your delivery is certain to be enthusiastic and lively.

7. **Vary Your Speaking Rate:** Your words should not be too fast or too slow. If you speak too slowly you will bore your audience. If you speak too rapidly you will be difficult to understand. Adapt your rate to the context of your speech. For example, if you are explaining complex information, slow down. If you are happy or enthusiastic, you should speed up. This "change of pace" is as important to a speaker as it is to a major-league baseball pitcher.

8. **Practice:** You now know the basic principles of effective delivery and should realize that the actual delivery of your presentation is just as important as having a well organized and developed speech. However, studying this information won't guarantee an effective speech presentation. You *must* rehearse and practice the speech you have prepared.

For best results, you should begin practicing several days before your actual presentation in class. Here are a few suggestions to help you when rehearsing.

a. Choose a location that will give you privacy and is free from distractions (an empty classroom or office at school; a bedroom or den at home where you can close the door). Don't practice in your living room while family members are watching TV or listening to music.

b. Allow yourself enough time to rehearse your speech from *start to finish*. It is not effective to practice just part of your speech during any one rehearsal session.

c. Practice your speech in front of a full-length mirror. This gives you an opportunity to monitor your eye contact and other aspects of delivery previously discussed.

d. Tape record yourself while rehearsing. As you play back the recording of your speech, be sure to listen for errors in content and delivery. Write down any corrections and work on improving them during your next practice session.

e. Practice your speech in front of a few friends or family members. Pretend that you are actually delivering your speech in front of your classmates. Ask your "audience" to comment on various aspects of your delivery.

Now you have suggestions for delivering your speeches as well as a variety of topics to talk about. So—let's get started with the business of speech making!

Confidence Building Speech #2:

SPEECH DESCRIBING A PERSONAL EXPERIENCE

GUIDELINES:

Due Date for Speech: _____

Time Limit: 2–3 minutes   (Practice it at home and time yourself.)

Preparing the Personal Experience Speech

We have all had many different kinds of experiences in our lifetime that we will never forget. We have all had:

An Embarrassing Experience	A Frightening Experience
A Funny Experience	An Interesting Experience
A Happy Experience	A Unique Experience
An Uncomfortable Experience	A Sad Experience
An Educational Experience	An Exciting Experience
A Dangerous Experience	A Surprising Experience

We've had our experiences at home, on the job, at school, in foreign countries, meeting new people, in parks, cars, airplanes, etc. We've had experiences with strangers, teachers, friends, and our family. We've had personal experiences as small children, teenagers, and now as college students.

ASSIGNMENT A

1. Choose a personal experience you have had as an adult.

2. Prepare an interesting speech to present about your experience.

3. Include all important details that will help your audience *feel* and *understand* your experience.

Some Details You Might Tell Include:

a. where you were

b. who was with you

c. what you were doing

d. what other people were doing

e. what you were feeling

f. why you felt the way you did

g. exactly what happened

h. how you reacted

i. why you will never forget this experience

Remember, your job is to make the audience relive your experience with you. If you had a happy experience, you must make us feel happy. If you had a sad experience, you must make us feel sad. If you had a scary experience, we should feel afraid. If you had a funny experience, we should laugh! *You must make us feel what you felt!*

SAMPLE SPEECH DESCRIBING A PERSONAL EXPERIENCE AS AN ADULT

One of our students, Francisco, made an adulthood experience speech that we have never forgotten. Here are some sections of his speech:

Introduction

Do you think it is possible to have an experience which is dangerous, happy, sad, uncomfortable, and very scary at the same time? I did, and I'll never forget it for the rest of my life.

Body

I escaped from Cuba three years ago at the age of 18 with my 15-year-old brother José. My father wanted us to live in a free country, get good educations, and have many opportunities. In Cuba, there was no hope for a good future. My father put José and me in an old leaking rowboat in the middle of the night. He told us that a city called Key West in the United States was only about ninety miles north of Cuba. Our trip from Havana to Key West took three days. We were all alone without food or water. I thought we were going to die. I tried to comfort my brother José by telling him how much better our lives would be when we finally got to Miami. I made myself feel better by thinking that we would go to heaven and meet my parents there one day. By some miracle, we finally got to Key West. Relatives of ours in Miami were notified by the immigration authorities and we went to live with them. After two years, we saw our parents again. They finally escaped from Cuba also. That was a very happy day for me.

Conclusion

Now that you know my experience, I think you can understand why it was scary, sad, dangerous, uncomfortable, and finally happy all at the same time. I didn't know it then but it was also the most important personal experience of my life. It was important because without that experience, I wouldn't be here today in a free and wonderful country talking to all of you. Thank you.

ASSIGNMENT B

1. Choose an incident or personal experience you had as a child.

2. Prepare a speech about this incident or experience. (This should be an easy speech for you to give. Just think back to your childhood and choose an event or experience you remember well. We have all done good, bad, interesting, and crazy things when we were children.)

3. Tell your audience what it was and then describe what happened to you. Include all details that will help the listeners relive this event with you.

Some Possible Childhood Experiences

a. The Time I Was Lost

b. My Most Memorable Birthday

c. My First Bicycle

d. A Terrible Lie I Told

e. My First Pet

f. My First Childhood Sweetheart

g. The Day I Played Hookey

h. The Night I Ran Away from Home

i. An Important Lesson I Learned

j. Convincing My Parents to Let Me Wear Lipstick

Remember, whether your teacher gives you Assignment A, Assignment B, or both, your job is to make the audience relive your experience with you.

SAMPLE SPEECH DESCRIBING A CHILDHOOD EXPERIENCE

A Malaysian student of ours made a very entertaining and interesting childhood experience speech that we remember well. Here are some sections of her speech.

Introduction

In my hands I have a jar of honey. If you look closely, you can see part of the honey beehive in the jar. You are probably wondering why I brought a jar of honey to show you today. Every time I see honey, it reminds me of a "stinging" experience I had when I was in the sixth grade.

Body

As a child I grew up on a farm not far from Kuala Lumpur, Malaysia. One warm summer day my friend and I were walking home from school. We happened to see a beehive in a tree. We had just studied in school about bee colonies and how bees make honey. This was my big chance to show off to my mother and father about what I learned in school.

It looked easy! I found a stick about two meters long. I handed it to my friend and told her to sneak up to the tree and hit the hive with the stick. I said I would wait until the bees came out and then I could grab the hive and run away with it.

I soon learned a very important lesson. I learned that things don't always work out the way you plan them. My friend pushed the hive down from the tree, and then ran at full speed up a nearby hill. The bees did not go after her. However, they were all over me instantly. They stung my arms; they flew down my blouse and stung me. They flew up my skirt and stung me; they got in my hair and stung me.

Conclusion

That was the first and last beehive that I have ever touched! Maybe now you can understand why this jar of honey I brought to show you reminds me of a very "stinging" experience!

Bring something to class that has special meaning for you. It can be anything—a painting, picture, item of clothing, piece of jewelry, or any other object. Be prepared to make a short speech about it. In your speech you should:

I. Describe what you brought to class. You might give the audience information like:

a. What is it?

b. Where is it from?

c. When did you get it?

d. How did you get it?

e. Who gave it to you?

f. How old is it?

g. What is it made of?

II. Describe why it has special meaning for you. You might tell the listeners:

a. Why do you like it?

b. Why is it important to you?

c. When did you discover it?

d. Why do you feel strongly about it?

e. Why do you want to share it with the class?

SAMPLE SPEECH ABOUT SOMETHING MEANINGFUL

A Navajo Indian student of ours from a reservation in Arizona made a very touching speech about an object that had special meaning for him. Here are some sections of his speech.

Introduction

In my hand I have an object in which spirits live! They float through bluish green stone and live forever. Would you like to see the object in which spirits live? I'll now show it to you.

Body

This is a turquoise gemstone. It is from the southwestern United States. My father gave this to me when I was a child. We were living in our hogan on the Navajo reservation.

This turquoise stone was first polished by my grandfather when he was a young man in the summer of 1831. I want you to know that turquoise is a mineral of aluminum and copper; when it is polished it becomes a brilliant bluish green gemstone.

This turquoise has a very special meaning for me because it represents the Navajo way of life. For the Navajo, all things of our earth contain the spirits of all the life forms that have touched them. When I look at this stone, its spirits help my mind to see scenes from the past: my grandfather's mud hogan, white flocks of sheep, the cedar wood fires, our struggle for survival, the desert in the summer, desert flowers and cactus, the human spirit of the Navajo. All these things belong to me in the memory of this stone.

Conclusion

I wanted to share this turquoise stone with all of you because we all need to realize that man must work with nature to change life for the better. I think you now understand why this magnificent object has special meaning for me. In this gemstone many wonderful memories and spirits from the past live again.

Confidence Building Speech #4:

SPEECH TO PRESENT A PERSONAL OPINION

GUIDELINES:

Due Date for Speech: _____

Time Limit: 2–3 minutes   (Practice it at home and time yourself.)

Certain issues, situations, attitudes, or points of view make us feel angry or worried, while we might agree with others. Every day we express our feelings about various topics to friends, family members, and others. We all have opinions about many different subjects. For example, you and your classmates probably feel strongly about one or more of the following:

Cruelty to Animals	Learning a Second Language
Preventing Child Abuse	Reducing Crime
The School You Attend	Achieving World Peace
Bringing Up Children	Drunken Drivers
Dishonest People	Drugs
The City You Live In	Rude or Impolite People
Serving in Your Country's Military	How Criminals Should Be Punished

Preparing the Personal Opinion Speech

1. Choose a subject about which you have a strong opinion. It could be a person, place, controversial issue, government policy, or someone's behavior. It could be *anything* that makes you want to express your views.

2. Tell your audience what your opinion is and *why* you feel the way you do. (It's always effective to give a specific example.)

Remember, put a lot of emotion into your personal opinion speech. If you are angry about something, we should *feel* your anger. If you are sad, we should *feel* your sorrow. If you are worried, we should *feel* your concern. If you are pleased, we should *feel* your approval.

SAMPLE SPEECH PRESENTING A PERSONAL OPINION

Here are some sections of a speech made by a student from Iran. He had been in the United States approximately three years when he gave this presentation.

Introduction

The other day I heard an American student say, "All foreign students are the same! They can't understand me and I can't understand them." This comment bothered me. In my opinion, American students should give other people a chance and not assume all students from other countries are alike.

Body

I believe that all people are unique and different. We all look different, we like different foods, some of us are shy and some are brave, and we all have different good and bad things about us. I say that just because we don't speak perfect English yet, all foreign students are not the same. I may be from another country but I understand what Americans say and every day I'm learning to speak English much better. People should not jump to conclusions about other people. We all must learn to be patient and give each person a chance.

Conclusion

Foreign students can not be put together and called the same. American students are not the same either. We are all different and we all have our own problems to face and solve. We must all learn to be more patient with one another and realize that no one is perfect. That's my opinion!

Confidence Building Speech #5:

SPEECH DESCRIBING A SPECIFIC FEAR

GUIDELINES:

Due Date for Speech: _____

Time Limit: 2–3 minutes   (Practice it at home and time yourself.)

Preparing the Speech to Describe a Specific Fear

We all have some fears and worries about something or someone. It is often helpful to talk about our fears and to hear other people talk about theirs. You might be surprised to learn that others are afraid of the same thing you are afraid of! For example, many people have a fear of:

Flying in Planes	Being in the Dark
Public Speaking	Going to a New Country
Meeting New People	Interviewing for a Job
Snakes	Large Dogs
Taking Tests	Going to Hospitals

1. Choose a personal fear that you have.

2. Prepare a speech about your fear to present to the class.

3. Include all important details that will help your audience *really understand* your fear and the reasons for it.

Some Details You Might Tell Include:

a. How old were you when this fear first developed?

b. What caused you to develop this fear?

c. How do you react when faced with this fearful situation?

d. What do your friends and family say about this fear of yours?

e. Have you ever tried to overcome this fear? If so, how? If not, why not?

Remember, it is perfectly normal to have a fear of some type. Anyone who says, "I'm not afraid of anything" is not telling the truth! The ability to talk about something you are afraid of and share your feelings with the class is a good way to help you gain confidence when speaking before an audience.

SAMPLE SPEECH DESCRIBING A SPECIFIC FEAR

Here are some sections of a speech made by a student from Mexico. Humberto had flown in single-engine airplanes.

Introduction

The earth was far below us. The weather was very bad. I looked at the instrument panel of the plane and saw a red warning light flashing. The pilot was very nervous. At that moment, the engine of the plane became silent!

Body

This happened to me last year when I was flying from Cancún to Cozumel in the Yucatán, Mexico. I will explain exactly what happened so you can understand why I now have a great fear of flying in planes.

Right after we took off from the airport in Cancún, the weather turned very bad. There was a lot of thunder and lightning. It was raining very hard. It was impossible for the pilot to see out the windows of the plane. I was the only person in the plane with the pilot. After being in the air for fifteen minutes, the plane started to shake and make strange noises. All of a sudden the engine just stopped.

When red warning lights started flashing, I became very afraid. I began to tremble and was soaked with sweat. I remember thinking that my life was about to end. I thought about how young I was and knew I didn't want to die. All of a sudden, the engine started to work again. The pilot turned to me, smiled, and said, "*No te preocupes*!" (That means "Don't worry.")

My mother and father do not want me to fly in small planes ever again. They say I should fly on the big airlines or take a boat! I promised myself, from now on, I will do what they told me.

Conclusion

I don't think I will ever fly in a small plane again. I get upset every time I think about it. I know that I will never be able to overcome this fear.

● *PRONUNCIATION TIPS*

It's important to stress the correct syllable of words when speaking. Unfortunately, English doesn't use written accent marks the way other languages do to tell us which syllable to stress.

> *Pronunciation Tip:* Compound nouns are usually stressed on the *first* part of the word, not the second.

There are hundreds of compound nouns in English. The above tip should be very useful to you.

EXERCISE A: Practice saying the following compound nouns aloud. Be sure to accent (say it louder) the *FIRST* part of the word.

bedroom	**school**house	**stop**sign
ice cream	**foot**ball	**book**store
baseball	**air**plane	**green**bean
grapefruit	**key**hole	**suit**case
drugstore	**cuff**link	**doll**house
bluebird	**sun**tan	**light**bulb

EXERCISE B: Try to think of ten more compound nouns.

1. _____   6. _____

2. _____   7. _____

3. _____   8. _____

4. _____   9. _____

5. _____   10. _____

EXERCISE C: Use Exercise A and B words in sentences. Say the sentences aloud. Be sure to stress the first part of all compound nouns.

2 *Thinking on Your Feet*

WHAT DO WE MEAN BY "THINKING ON YOUR FEET"?

Of course, thinking is something we do all day long whether we are working or playing, sitting in a chair or standing on our feet. When we say "thinking on your feet" we are talking about the need to organize your ideas quickly and speak about a subject without being given advance time to prepare. This type of "thinking on your feet speech" has a name: *impromptu speaking*. You must organize your thoughts quickly and depend on what you already know and can think of to talk about on the spur of the moment.

WHEN DO WE MAKE IMPROMPTU SPEECHES?

Believe it or not, we make impromptu speeches all the time! Most of our conversations with friends, parents, teachers, employers, etc. are really short "thinking on your feet" talks. We make these talks at work, home, school, parties, etc. These impromptu talks might include answering questions, giving opinions, or sharing our knowledge about the many topics we discuss with people on a daily basis. So as you can see, you already have some experience and should find that making impromptu speeches is fun and easy!

CLASSROOM ACTIVITY I

Your teacher will call on different students in the class to answer the following questions. When it's your turn, pretend your response is a short "impromptu" speech. Be sure to tell *why* you feel the way you do by giving the class examples and reasons for your opinion.

1. Do you like to travel?

2. Describe the best teacher you've ever had.

3. Should there be laws against cigarette smoking in public places?

4. Explain a custom in your country which is different from customs in other countries.

5. What do you look for in a friend?

6. Do you have a favorite holiday?

7. Of all the places you have ever been, which is your favorite?

8. Why do people get married?

9. Should a woman be the president or leader of a country?

10. Should women with small children have jobs outside of the home?

11. What do you like best about living in this country?

12. Do you miss your country?

13. Should an unmarried person be allowed to adopt a child?

14. How do you feel about divorce?

15. What is your favorite time of year?

16. Should women have the same rights as men?

17. How do you feel about capital punishment?

18. What should the legal drinking age be?

19. Do you think television can be harmful to children?

20. What do you think about countries that refuse to participate in the Olympics?

21. In your country, what do you do in your free time?

22. Do you believe in extrasensory perception?

23. Is it important to learn to speak more than one language?

24. Can child abuse be prevented?

25. Do you feel there should be laws against people owning handguns?

CLASSROOM ACTIVITY II

Good impromptu speakers are accustomed to elaborating on their thoughts without being prompted. Although not directly asked for specific information, they can anticipate what the listener might be interested in and provide it effortlessly. To give you practice in this, your teacher will ask you questions which appear to request a simple "yes" or "no" response. Go deeper than the surface and expand your response. The following example illustrates:

QUESTION: Do you go to school?

ANSWER 1: Yes. (This is a superficial response.)

ANSWER 2: Yes. I'm a junior at XYZ University and I'm majoring in business administration. (This is a good response. The speaker found the hidden or implied part to the "yes/no" question asked.)

1. Do you work?

2. Are you an only child?

3. Do you live near here?

4. Do you like animals?

5. Is summer your favorite season?

6. Are you taking other classes?

7. Do you live alone?

8. Did you study English before coming here?

9. Do you have any pets?

10. Are you a good cook?

11. Do you have any siblings?

12. Do you drive?

13. Is math an easy subject for you?

14. Do you watch TV?

15. Do you go to the movies?

16. Is this class interesting?

Preparing for the Impromptu Speech

The best preparation for an impromptu speech is to be well informed about people, places, and news events happening in your city, state, around the country, and even around the world. This type of information will give you many topics of conversation to talk about with people in many different situations.

FOR HOMEWORK

The following activities will help you become better informed and able to speak about many subjects when asked to make impromptu talks. Your teacher will assign some of these for homework and ask you to talk about them in class.

1. **Watch the evening news on TV.** Be prepared to describe the details of a news story to the class.

2. **Listen to a radio news station for 10 minutes.** Choose a news item that you found very interesting and describe it to the class. Explain why you feel this is an interesting story.

3. **Read the editorial page of your local newspaper.** Choose one of the controversial issues written about and be ready to tell why you agree or disagree with the editor's opinions.

4. **Look through a national newsmagazine like *Time*, *Newsweek*, or *U.S. News and World Report*.** Choose an article you feel is very important. Be prepared to talk about the article in class and explain why it contains information which is important for everyone to know about.

5. **Describe a news event to three different people** (outside of class). Ask them their opinions about what you read or heard. Be ready to discuss your friends' opinions and why they feel the way they do about the issue or news story.

Another excellent way to prepare for an impromptu speech is to learn different methods to develop and organize your thoughts. If you are prepared with a variety of possible ways to approach an unknown topic, you will find your information easy to understand and remember.

The following are methods you might choose to organize your ideas for an impromptu speech. Your teacher will discuss these and answer your questions. However, when the time comes to make an impromptu presentation, you will have to decide which of these is the best method to use for *your particular topic.*

Impromptu Speech Approaches

1. Past—Present—Future Sequence

This approach can be used to discuss how events, issues, customs, technology, etc. once were, how they have changed or improved, and how they will be in the future.

EXAMPLE: In discussing "The Olympics" you might organize your information under the following three headings:

    I. The History of the Olympics

    II. The Olympics Today

    III. The Future of the Olympic Games

2. Time Sequence

This approach can be used to describe how processes, personal experiences, events, activities, etc. happen by the hour, part of the day, week, month, year, etc. It can also be used to explain the proper order of steps to follow to complete an activity.

EXAMPLE: In speaking about "Making a Speech" you might organize your information under the following headings:

    I. Choosing A Topic

    II. Gathering Information

    III. Making an Outline

    IV. Presenting the Speech

3. Cause–Effect Sequence

This approach can be used to discuss and describe a particular problem, event or situation that exists (inflation, high school drop-outs, divorce, crime, unemployment, discrimination, fuel shortages) and then talk about the effects or results this problem or event may create.

EXAMPLE: When presented with the topic "Cigarette Smoking" you might discuss:

    I. The effects of smoking on the heart

    II. The effects of smoking on the lungs

    III. The effects of smoking on other parts of the body

4. Effect–Causes Sequence

This approach can be used to describe a particular event or problem (as described in #3 above) and then talk about what things caused this event or situation to take place.

EXAMPLE: In speaking about "Drug Addiction" you might discuss reasons that people become addicted to drugs in the first place, i.e.:

    I. Easy availability of drugs

    II. The need to escape from the pressures and tensions of work

    III. Lack of education about harmful effects of drugs

5. Problem—Solution Sequence

This approach can be used to speak about a specific problem that exists in your community or in society in general (similar to the "causes" in #3). After describing the problem, you should then suggest ways to reduce it or solve it.

> *Note:* The "problems" aren't always negative situations like crime, child abuse, poverty, etc. They could be problems that occur in the process of daily living ("Choosing a Career," "Selecting a College," "Deciding Where to Go on Vacation," etc.).

EXAMPLE: In speaking about the problem of "Choosing the College That's Right For You," you might present the following solutions:

I. Read the different college catalogues

II. Visit campuses of different colleges

III. Talk to people who attend various colleges

IV. Talk to teachers at the colleges you are considering

6. Geographical Sequence

This approach can be used to discuss topics according to different geographical areas and locations. Your topic might be considered by city, state, country, continent, or planet!

EXAMPLE: In speaking about "Interesting Marriage Customs" you might use the following geographical sequence:

I. Marriage Customs in Japan

II. Marriage Customs in Saudi Arabia

III. Marriage Customs in the United States

7. Related Subtopic Sequence

This approach can be used to divide a topic into different parts or subtopics. The parts are related because they all belong to the same original topic.

EXAMPLE: You might divide the subject of "Advertising" into the following sub-topics:

    I. Television Advertising

    II. Magazine Advertising

    III. Radio Advertising

8. Advantage—Disadvantage Sequence

This approach can be used to talk about both positive and negative aspects of a topic or issue. It consists of a balanced discussion of both advantages and disadvantages. When using this approach, try to be as objective as possible and avoid giving your personal opinion.

EXAMPLE: If you used this approach when speaking about "The Death Penalty" you might first discuss reasons why it is good for society to have capital punishment and then reasons why it is bad to have capital punishment. Your two main headings would be:

    I. Advantages of Capital Punishment

    II. Disadvantages of Capital Punishment

9. Personal Opinion Approach

This approach can be used to discuss a topic you have strong feelings about. When using the personal opinion approach you should develop it with examples and reasons which support *why* you feel the way you do.

EXAMPLE: In talking about "Gambling," you might choose to present your opinion that casino gambling should not be legal. Remember, you must give the audience the different reasons which explain why you feel as you do.

10. Personal Experience Approach

This approach can be used to tell a story about an experience you had which is related to the topic. Be sure to describe the details which will help your listeners understand exactly what happened to you or what you learned from the experience.

EXAMPLE: In talking about "Discrimination" you might describe a situation in which you were the object of some type of discrimination. Or, you might explain how you discriminated against someone else and learned an important lesson as a result.

11. Special Approach of Your Own Choice

The special approach is one that you think of by yourself. Maybe you can come up with a completely different (but organized) way to approach your topic. Be creative and use your imagination!

REVIEW TEST

On the line to the left of each number, write the letter of the choice which best shows the approach the speaker has decided to use.

a. Geographical Sequence

b. Effect–Causes Sequence

c. Past–Present–Future Sequence

d. Problem–Solution Sequence

e. Time Sequence

f. Related Subtopic Sequence

g. Personal Experience Approach

h. Advantage-Disadvantage Sequence

_____ 1. In a speech about "High School Drop-Outs," Mary presented a series of suggestions for parents and teachers to follow in order to help teenagers do well in high school. She also suggested that students should help and encourage each other to graduate from high school.

_____ 2. José also spoke about "High School Drop-Outs." However, he discussed many reasons which cause students to drop out of school. He pointed out that a) some students don't receive encouragement at home, b) they need money to help support their families so they leave school to get jobs, or c) they would rather "hang out" with friends than go to class.

_____ 3. Kim was asked to make a speech about "Looking for a Job." He explained that the first thing to do was to prepare a résumé of his experience. The second thing to do was to read the employment section in the paper or visit an employment agency. Kim said the last thing to do was to schedule job interviews and pray a lot!

_____ 4. Michelle made a speech about "Gambling." She chose three states in the United States where certain types of gambling are legal and described the different forms of gambling available in Florida, New York, and Nevada.

_____ 5. Jean spoke about "Automobiles." She described cars of sixty years ago and how hard they were to drive. She then talked about the automatic cars we have now with their many modern features. Finally, she said that some day our cars would be driven by computers and we will relax and enjoy the ride!

_____ 6. Claude was asked to speak about "Entertainment in Your City." He divided his subject into the following headings: _Entertainment for Music Lovers, Entertainment for Art Lovers, Entertainment for Theatre Lovers._

_____ 7. Kimiko's topic for a speech was "Pets." She spoke about the problems people have with pets as well as all the happiness and joy pets can give their owners.

_____ 8. Mohammed was asked to speak about "Gambling." He told about the time he lost all his money in a casino in Puerto Rico and didn't have enough money to go back home to Saudi Arabia.

_____ 9. Luisa spoke about "A Day in the Life of a Teacher." She organized her information under the following headings: _Early Morning Preparation, Classroom Teaching, After School Activities._

_____10. Hector was given the topic "Saving Money." He said that saving money was a problem because everything is very expensive. He suggested that some good ways to save money are to comparison shop for the best price, to buy things on sale, and to eat less expensive foods.

Impromptu Speech Outline

The following is an outline of an impromptu speech given by one of our students. In the actual speech, he gave a variety of specific examples and talked about friends and family members with the different addictions. So, although not complete, the following outline should give you a good idea about how one student organized his thoughts on the spur of the moment. Can you guess which type of approach was used to make this speech?

ADDICTIONS

Introduction

I. I bet everyone in this room knows an addict! That's right, I said *addict*. Before you get angry, please let me explain.

II. When we hear the word "addiction" we usually think of bad addictions like drugs or alcohol. We forget there are many other kinds of addictions. I'd now like to remind you of some.

Body

I. Television Addictions
   A. Soap Operas
   B. Detective Shows
   C. Football or Baseball

II. Book Addictions
   A. Romance Novels
   B. Mysteries
   C. Science Fiction

III. Eating Addictions
   A. Ice cream
   C. Chocolate

IV. Other Addictions
   A. Shopping (clothes, cars, antiques)
   B. Hobbies (stamp collection, photography, etc.)
   C. Sports (playing golf, tennis, jogging)

Conclusion

I. As you can see, you really do know someone who is an addict!

II. What kind of addict are you?

GRADED IMPROMPTU SPEECH PRESENTATION

You are now ready to make a real "thinking on your feet" speech in front of the class. Your teacher might assign you a topic to speak about or have you pick a subject card "out of a hat." Either way, you won't know your topic until the day of your speech. However, you will be given a few minutes to organize your thoughts and write down some ideas before you speak.

The following are possible impromptu speech topics. Your teacher will explain any terms you don't understand and may ask you to suggest other topics.

Impromptu Speech Topics

Travel

An Important Story in the News

Culture Shock

Mercy Killing

Learning English

The Working Student

Different Customs

Dishonesty

Capital Punishment

"Where There's a Will There's a Way"

Child Abuse

Gambling

Habits

Being on Time

Responsibilities

The Importance of Communication

Government Regulations

Hobbies

Discrimination

Women's Rights

Meeting People

Prostitution

On the day of your speech, your presentation will be evaluated. Some of the specific aspects of this speech that your teacher may critique include:

I. Speaking Voice
   A. Volume of Voice (Did you speak loud enough to be easily heard?)
   B. Rate of Speech (Did you speak slow enough to be clearly understood?)

II. The Speech
   A. Attention-Getting Introduction
   B. Clarity of Approach (Were the teacher and other students easily able to determine which of the impromptu speech approaches, as discussed in the chapter, were used?)
   C. Organization of Ideas
   D. Sufficient Support/Examples
   E. Graceful Conclusion

● *PRONUNCIATION TIPS*

In English, there are many nouns and verbs which look exactly alike when written. However, when spoken, we can distinguish between these word pairs through the use of stress.

> *Pronunciation Tip:* **The noun will always be stressed on the *FIRST* syllable; the verb should be stressed on the *SECOND* syllable.**

EXERCISE A: Practice saying the following noun/verb pairs aloud. Be sure to stress the noun on the **first** syllable and the verb on the **second**.

Nouns		*Verbs*	
present	(a gift)	pre**sent**	(to give; to show)
project	(a task; assignment)	pro**ject**	(to estimate or guess)
convict	(a criminal)	con**vict**	(to find guilty)
object	(a thing; purpose)	ob**ject**	(to oppose; disagree with)
record	(a written account; report; recording)	re**cord**	(to write down; register)

EXERCISE B: Read the following sentences aloud. Carefully pronounce the stress pattern differences between the italicized words in each sentence.

1. Please **recórd** the **récord**.
2. I **objéct** to that ugly **óbject**.
3. She will **presént** you with a **présent**.
4. We **projéct** that Mario will do a good **próject**.
5. The judge will **convíct** the **cónvict** again.

EXERCISE C: Read the following sentences aloud. On the line to the right of each sentence, (a) indicate whether the boldface word is a noun or a verb, and (b) circle the number of the syllable which should be stressed. (Your teacher will check your answers.)

Example: Enrique read "Reader's **Digest**." 　　noun _____

1. Inger likes ice cream for **desert**. 　　_____

2. The **convict** escaped from jail. 　　_____

3. They signed the **contract**. 　　_____

4. Never **desert** a friend in trouble. 　　_____

5. Don't **convict** me for something I didn't do. 　　_____

3 *Listening*

Listening is one of the most important and frequent behaviors we engage in. We all spend close to fifty percent of the time we are awake listening. As college students, you spend almost ninety percent of your school time listening. The following quotes prove that the value of good listening skills was identified thousands of years ago.

Know how to listen and you will profit even from those who talk badly.

Plutarch, Greek Historian

Nature has given to men one tongue but two ears, that we may hear from others twice as much as we speak.

Epictetus, Ancient Philosopher

Hearing is good and speaking is good, but he who hears is a possessor of benefits.

Ptahhotpe, Egyptian Vizier

The ability to listen is vital in all our lives. It is very important for all of us to improve our listening skills and be the best listeners we can be. This may seem simple, but it isn't as easy as it sounds. The exercises and activities in this chapter will give you listening practice in a variety of situations and help improve your ability to listen effectively.

We all know that it is important to listen carefully when teachers lecture, friends talk, parents or advisors provide information, bosses explain something, or radio commentators report the news. Unfortunately, we don't always pay attention when someone is speaking to us, although we know we should. We allow ourselves to be distracted and our minds wander. There are several bad listening habits which many people have. By knowing what they are, you can avoid them and become a better listener.

Common Bad Listening Habits and Their Cures

Bad Listening Habit #1: Being Distracted by the Speaker's Appearance/Delivery

You don't listen to what a speaker is saying because you are concentrating on his or her accent, speech patterns, gestures, posture, or how he or she looks, is dressed, etc.

Cure: Concentrate on what the speaker is saying, not on how he or she looks or sounds. You can miss important information by thinking about a person's appearance or delivery style instead of his or her words.

Bad Listening Habit #2: Deciding the Topic Is Boring

You decide in advance that you will be bored by what the speaker is going to talk about. Deciding that a subject is dull before you hear what a person has to say gives you an excuse not to listen. It's easy to take the attitude, "Why should I pay attention when I'm not interested in this?"

> **EXAMPLE:** The president of a local bank came to speak to the college students about inflation. You decided you weren't interested in the topic and would be bored so you brought a newspaper to read during the banker's speech. He made excellent suggestions about fighting inflation and saving money. All your friends thought it was a great speech with much useful information. *But you weren't listening!*

Cure: Never take the attitude, "I must sit through another boring talk." Even if you are uninterested in the topic at first, remember, some of the information could be important or interesting. Make an effort to listen for information that you could later use (in a college course, job, or conversation with friends or family). Adopt the attitude, "I may as well listen since I'm already here."

Bad Listening Habit #3: Faking Attention

You pretend to be listening but your mind is on other things. You might be looking directly at the speaker and even nodding your head in agreement, when you are actually daydreaming, thinking about your own problems, or planning what *you* want to say. The speaker thinks you are a polite and interested listener when you are really not paying any attention.

> **EXAMPLE:** Margaret Lane, author of a Reader's Digest article entitled, "Are You Really Listening?" describes how faking attention cost her a job: When interviewing for a job on a newspaper, the editor described his winter ski trip. She wanted to impress him by talking about a camping trip in the same mountains and started planning her own adventure story. The editor suddenly asked, "What do you think of that?" Ms. Lane (not having listened to him) answered, "Sounds like fun!" The annoyed editor replied, "Fun? I just told you I was in the hospital with a broken leg."

Cure: Stop pretending to pay attention. Be sincere and take a real interest in the person speaking to you. If you are too busy to listen, and must use the time to think about other things, be honest! Ask the speaker if he or she can tell you later when you can really take the time to listen.

Bad Listening Habit #4: Looking for Distractions

You allow yourself to be distracted by your surroundings. You might look out the window, look at the cracked or peeling paint on the wall, play with a pencil or hair clip, look at how people in the room are dressed, etc.

> **EXAMPLE:** One of our students failed a math test because she wasn't listening when the teacher told the class to be prepared for a quiz the following day. She was looking at the boy with dandruff seated in front of her and was thinking how ugly his hair looked.

Cure: Concentrate! Refuse to allow distractions to take your mind off the speaker. There will always be distractions wherever you are. Have willpower—ignore them!

Bad Listening Habit #5: Overconcentrating on Unimportant Facts

You concentrate too much on a specific fact or detail and forget to listen to the speaker's important points or ideas. You might spend too much time thinking about an unimportant piece of information and suddenly realize you missed more important information.

EXAMPLE:

ADVISOR: "On Friday, May 10, Miss Martin, the Director of Financial Aid, spoke about How to Apply for a Scholarship."

STUDENT: "May 10th was a Thursday, not a Friday."

ADVISOR: "I'll now summarize this important information for you. . . ."

STUDENT: "It's not Miss Martin, it's Mrs. Martin."

ADVISOR: "Write to the address I gave you and send the application."

STUDENT: "What address? What application?"

Cure: When listening, pay attention to the general purpose of the message rather than to specific facts. Remember, speakers want you to understand their main ideas more than insignificant details they might mention. Listen for the main point of the talk first, then take note of any supporting facts.

Bad Listening Habit #6: Reacting Emotionally to Trigger Words

You ignore or distort what a speaker is saying because you react emotionally to trigger words. A "trigger" is a word which causes you to have an emotional (negative or positive) reaction of some kind. Certain words will cause you to remember specific feelings and experiences. When this happens, your ability to listen decreases because you allow your emotions to take over. When a person's favorite subject is mentioned, he or she might begin thinking about it and want to express personal opinions. If an unpleasant subject is mentioned, some people get upset or angry and stop listening to what the speaker is saying.

EXAMPLE 1: Pilar, a student from Argentina, was listening to her economics professor discuss "The Economy in South America." As soon as he mentioned Buenos Aires, Pilar became homesick and started to think about her friends and family still there. The mention of Buenos Aires caused her to have a pleasant emotional reaction. However, pleasant or not, the trigger word "Buenos Aires" caused Pilar to stop listening to her teacher's lecture.

EXAMPLE 2: Several students have reported that "nuclear weapons" or "nuclear arms race" are their emotional trigger words. Upon hearing newscasters say these words, they become so preoccupied with the possibility of World War III that they stop listening to the rest of the newscast even though the commentator started to discuss other topics.

Cure: Identify a variety of "trigger" words, topics, names of people which affect *you* personally. Once you determine what they are, you can reduce their effect on you by recognizing them as soon as they are said. This will help you to remain objective and concentrate on the speaker's message. Let the speaker finish what he or she is saying before you allow past memories to cause you to react emotionally. The following classroom activity will help you identify your "emotional triggers."

CLASSROOM ACTIVITY

Your teacher will organize you into small groups of three to four students. Identify any words, people, or topics which cause you to have a strong positive or negative reaction. Discuss these within your group. You may find that others have the same "emotional triggers" as you. Each of you should complete the emotional trigger box below. Think of as many as you can in each category. Be prepared to discuss with the class how these words, topics, or people's names cause you to react emotionally and stop listening when you hear them.

Emotional Triggers Which Block Effective Listening

	Negative	Positive
WORDS		
PEOPLE		
SUBJECTS		

REVIEW TEST

On the line to the left of each number, write the letter of the choice which best shows the common bad listening habit being displayed.

a. *Being Distracted by Speaker's Appearance/Delivery*

b. *Deciding the Topic is Boring*

c. *Faking Attention*

d. *Looking for Distractions*

e. *Overconcentration on Facts*

f. *Reacting to Emotional Triggers*

_____ 1. A Mexican tour guide was explaining the history of Chapultepec Castle to some American tourists. One of the tourists loved to hear the way Spanish speakers roll their R's and paid more attention to the guide's pronunciation than to his explanation.

_____ 2. Linda was doing a crossword puzzle when her friend Rosa telephoned. As Rosa was talking, Linda kept saying "Really" and "I see" to make Rosa think she was listening. Linda was really working on her crossword puzzle.

_____ 3. Akiko's physical education teacher was explaining how to save the life of a heart attack victim through the use of CPR. As the teacher was speaking, Akiko was saddened by the memory of her grandfather who recently died of a heart attack. All she could think about was the good times they had together before he died.

_____ 4. Your friend is teaching you how to use his new camera. You want to learn to use the camera but you notice he just bought an expensive stereo system with four speakers. While he is talking, you are looking at his new stereo wishing you could afford one also.

_____ 5. Nachum, an Israeli student, told us that whenever the subject of the World War II Holocaust is mentioned, he gets very upset and emotional. He immediately thinks of his grandparents, who died in a concentration camp; he is completely unable to listen to the speaker or follow the rest of the conversation.

_____ 6. A counselor was speaking about college graduation requirements. Lena decided that she didn't need to listen and would look up the information in the college catalog. She wrote a letter to her boyfriend instead of listening to the speaker. She missed valuable information about new requirements which were not printed in the catalog.

_____ 7. Your aunt is not a stylish dresser. You never really listen to what she says because when you see her you think about how her blouse doesn't match her skirt or how old-fashioned-looking her dress is.

_____ 8. A group of people were listening to a book review at their local library. One man was concentrating on remembering the exact ages and birthdates of all the characters; unfortunately, he missed much of the librarian's fascinating description of the spy novel's general plot.

LISTENING TEST I

Answer Form

Your teacher will read six different fact groups, each followed by two or three statements. Based on the information contained in the fact group, indicate whether each related statement is **fact** or **opinion** by checking the correct box.

EXAMPLE FACT GROUP: Girls are never named Richard. Richard is a popular male name. Rick, Richie, and Dick are common nicknames for boys and men named Richard.

		Fact	Opinion
Statement (a):	Only males are named Richard.	☒	☐
Statement (b):	Ricky is a nicer nickname than Dick or Richie.	☐	☒
Fact Group A:	Statement 1:	☐	☐
	Statement 2:	☐	☐
	Statement 3:	☐	☐
Fact Group B:	Statement 4:	☐	☐
	Statement 5:	☐	☐
	Statement 6:	☐	☐
Fact Group C:	Statement 7:	☐	☐
	Statement 8:	☐	☐
	Statement 9:	☐	☐
Fact Group D:	Statement 10:	☐	☐
	Statement 11:	☐	☐
Fact Group E:	Statement 12:	☐	☐
	Statement 13:	☐	☐
Fact Group F:	Statement 14:	☐	☐
	Statement 15:	☐	☐

LISTENING TEST 2

Answer Form

Listen carefully as your teacher reads the following passages about the heart. Fill in the blanks with the missing nouns.

The heart is a powerful _____ located in the _____ directly under the breast _____. The heart of _____ and other _____ and of birds is divided into four _____. They are the left and right auricles and the left and right ventricles. The auricles receive _____ from the _____ and push it into the ventricles. The _____ pump the blood out of the _____ and around the _____.

Beating is an automatic _____ of the heart. It begins early in embryonic _____ before the _____ is born, and continues without stopping throughout _____. All body _____ constantly need _____ which is carried to them by the circulating _____. If a person's heart stops beating for a few _____, unconsciousness will result. _____ will occur if it stops for a few _____. A resting person's heart pumps about five _____ of blood per minute. In seventy _____ a human's _____ beats about two billion six hundred million times. The number of _____ per minute and the amount of _____ pumped are greatly increased during _____.

The heart is able to continue beating after its _____ have been cut. In fact, if it is kept in the proper type of _____, it will beat even when entirely removed from the _____!

LISTENING TEST 3

Answer Form

Listen carefully as your teacher reads the following passage about water. Fill in the blanks with the missing verbs.

     Water _____ the most precious of all the resources on earth. Without water, no plant, animal, or any form of life could have _____. Believe it or not, every drop of water on earth when earth _____ _____ _____ on our planet even now. Water is always _____. It _____ _____ around the globe many times. The heat of the sun _____ it from the oceans. It is _____ along in clouds by winds. Water _____ from the sky in the form of rain, snow, hail or sleet. It _____ _____ for hundreds of years in ice caps and glaciers or _____ back to the sea through storm sewers and rivers. Almost all the water on earth _____ in the oceans. No one is exactly certain, but scientists _____ that life itself _____ in the sea about three billion years ago.

LISTENING TEST 4

Answer Form

Listen carefully as your teacher reads the article entitled "Lying: Studies in Deception." Based on the reading, decide whether the following statements are true or false. (Circle the correct answer.)

True **False**   1. The ability to lie well is not a simple skill to learn.

True **False**   2. An expert can easily detect a good liar.

True **False**   3. Many companies and government agencies use polygraph tests each year.

True False   4. Most experts agree that polygraph or lie detector tests are reliable.

True False   5. Several thousand publications contend that lie detector tests are accurate.

True False   6. People have only recently become interested in attempting to detect lies.

LISTENING TEST 5

Answer Form

Listen carefully as your teacher reads the passage about "Daydreaming." Based on the reading, decide whether the following statements are true or false. (Circle the correct answer.)

True False   1. Almost everyone daydreams or fantasizes daily.

True False   2. Most daydreams are unrealistic and bizarre.

True False   3. Daydreaming is a perfectly normal and enjoyable activity.

True False   4. Women daydream or fantasize more than men.

True False   5. The older generation daydreams less than the younger generation.

True False   6. It is not normal for children to engage in fantasy play.

True False   7. Although daydreaming has several advantages, it can be harmful.

LISTENING TEST 6

Answer Form

Listen carefully to your teacher's oral reading. Based on the reading, answer the following questions.

1. Where did the young man sit down?

_____

2. Who started the conversation?

_____

3. How old did the old woman feel?

_____

4. What did the young man say?

_____

5. Did the old woman agree with what the young man said? Why?

_____

LISTENING TEST 7

Answer Form

Listen carefully to your teacher's oral reading. Based on the reading, answer the following questions.

1. Where did the businessman go one afternoon?

_____

2. What was wrong with the businessman?

_____

3. How long did the bartender know the businessman?

_____

4. What did the bartender tell the businessman?

_____

5. How did the businessman answer?

_____

6. What was the bartender's final remark?

_____

7. What is your opinion about the bartender's final statement?

_____

LISTENING TEST 8

Answer Form

Listen carefully to your teacher's oral reading. Based on what you hear, answer the following questions.

1. Who was the first person to have an umbrella?

   _____

2. What was this first umbrella made of?

   _____

3. What is the derivation* and meaning of the word "umbrella"?

   _____

4. When did people start using umbrellas in the rain?

   _____

5. What were umbrella ribs made of in the early 1900's?

   _____

6. What are umbrellas made of today?

   _____

7. What kind of umbrella has not yet been invented?

   _____

8. Which companies claim they find more lost umbrellas than anything else?

   _____

*derivation = where does it come from?

LISTENING TEST 9

Answer Form

Listen carefully to the questions or directions your teacher will read for each item. After listening to the instructions for an item, respond to that item on your answer form in the appropriate manner.

1. 2   5   17   20   24   100   59

2. red   blue   chair   green   desk   table   black   seven   twenty

3. W   B   X   E   Z   C   U

4.

5.

6. apple   pear   corn   carrot   banana   paper   squash

7.

8.

9.

10.

• PRONUNCIATION TIPS

In English, the majority of words end in consonant sounds. In many other languages, however, the majority of words end in vowels. Because you might not be used to using final consonants in your native language, you might frequently omit them at the ends of words in English. Without realizing it, you can confuse your listeners and they will have trouble understanding you.

> **Pronunciation Tip:** Pronounce final consonants **carefully.** (Although "e" may be the last letter in a word, it is usually silent; a **consonant** is actually the last sound.)
>
> **Examples:** ma**de** pho**ne** bi**te** ha**ve**

EXERCISE A: The words in each of the following rows will sound the same if their final consonant sound is left off. Read each row aloud. **Exaggerate** your pronunciation of the final consonant in each word.

1. ca**t** ca**p** ca**b** ca**n** ca**lf**
2. rac**k** ra**t** ra**p** ra**g** ra**n**
3. sou**p** soo**n** sui**t** sue**d** Sue**'s**
4. wee**k** wee**p** whea**t** wee**d** wea**ve**
5. ro**be** ro**de** wro**te** ro**pe** ro**ll**

EXERCISE B: Read the following sentences aloud. **Exaggerate** your pronunciation of the final consonant in each boldface word.

1. Ha**ve** you ha**d** ha**m**?
2. I li**ke** bright lig**ht**.
3. The sig**n** is on the si**de**.
4. Dou**g** ate a well do**ne** du**ck**.
5. The ba**g** on his bac**k** was blac**k**.

EXERCISE C: Choose any paragraph in this book. Circle all words that end in consonant sounds. Read the paragraph aloud; **be sure to pronounce all final consonant sounds**. (Your teacher will be there to remind you.)

4 *Putting Your Speech Together*

"Where do I begin?" is a common question often asked by students faced with the task of writing a speech. This chapter will help you learn to organize and outline your thoughts and information to enable you to deliver your speech logically and clearly.

EVERY SPEECH NEEDS A SUBJECT AND A PURPOSE

Before you can begin gathering and organizing information for your speech, you must select a topic and clearly understand its purpose. For example, your purpose might be to inform people about an unfamiliar subject, or to persuade them to change their opinion about an issue. Chapters 5 and 7 contain valuable information which will help you to choose a subject and understand your specific purpose.

EVERY SPEECH HAS THREE PARTS

I. *Introduction*   (the opening of a speech)

II. *Body*   (the middle or main part of a speech)

III. *Conclusion*   (the ending of a speech)

The question is, "Which part of a speech do you prepare first?" The following mini-quiz will determine if you know the answer. Be careful—the answer may surprise you!

MINI-QUIZ

Use the numbers 1, 2, or 3 to indicate which of the following you would do first, second, and last.

a. ____ Prepare the introduction or opening of your speech.

b. ____ Prepare the body or main part of your speech.

c. ____ Prepare the conclusion or ending of your speech.

The correct answers are b, c, a! You should begin with the body of your speech. After the body is prepared, you should write the conclusion, and finally the introduction. So, every speech you give in this class should be prepared as follows:

First:	The Body
Second:	The Conclusion
Third:	The Introduction

Step One: Preparing the Body of Your Speech

The body of your speech will contain the outline of the major ideas you want to present. It will also have the evidence or information that supports and clarifies your ideas.

First: List the Main Headings or Subtopics Related to Your Subject

Write down the main headings which might be included in your speech. Write them as you think of them. Some ideas will be important, some will be insignificant. At this time, just concentrate on writing all the ideas you can think of that relate to the subject and purpose of your speech.

Second: Narrow Down Your List of Main Headings

Review your list of main headings carefully. Your goal should be to come up with the three or four main headings that will develop the subject and purpose of your speech. For example: You are preparing a speech entitled "Having a Happy Marriage," and have thought of nine different subtopics. You must narrow your list to three or four of them. They might include:

I. Respect Your Spouse's Property

II. Always Be Courteous to One Another

III. Give Honest Appreciation

IV. Learn to Compromise

Third: Order Your Main Headings Logically

Try to organize your main headings so that each major point leads naturally into the next one. For example, if your speech were entitled "Applying for a Job," you would not talk about the actual interview before discussing the need for a résumé. A more logical order of main headings might be:

I. Finding the Desired Position

II. Writing a Résumé

III. Scheduling Appointments

IV. Behavior During the Personal Interview

Refer to "Chapter 2: Thinking on Your Feet" for detailed explanations about different ways to organize your speech.

Fourth: Develop Your Main Headings

The main headings are the skeleton upon which your speech will be built. You must develop and support them. If the main headings are properly supported by factual information, logical proof, and visuals, your audience will understand and remember your speech. Both Chapters 4 and 6 contain sections entitled "Gathering Information." Read these carefully to learn how to use your own knowledge, personal experiences, examples, quotes from experts, visual aids, and information from books, newspapers and magazines to develop your main headings. The section "Outlining" beginning on page 60 of this chapter will teach you how to organize and outline the information you gathered to develop the body of your speech.

Step Two: Preparing the Conclusion of Your Speech

The conclusion will contain a summary of what you spoke about as well as final remarks to end your speech gracefully. A good summary reminds your audience about what you said and helps them to remember your information. You may do this by briefly reviewing your purpose and repeating the main headings of your speech. After a summary, you are ready to conclude with a statement that will leave your audience thinking about what you said. The sections entitled "Preparing a Summary of What You Spoke About," and "Preparing a Memorable Conclusion" in Chapter 5 provide many examples of ways to conclude a speech.

Step Three: Preparing the Introduction to Your Speech

Your job is clear. You must introduce your topic, your purpose, and yourself to your audience in clear, short, and understandable sentences. A good introduction tells your audience that your speech is going to be interesting and worth listening to.

Begin your speech with a short, attention-getting sentence. For example:

> *It is a fact that slavery exists in fifteen nations of the world today.*

The above sentence is short and clear. The speaker shocked his audience and aroused their curiosity. What nations? Where are they? How does the speaker know this? This speaker made his audience want to listen to the rest of his speech.

Let's look at another example of a good introduction. Our student, Maylin, started her speech with a short, clear opener that told her audience what her speech was going to be about. She then developed her idea to make it more interesting:

> *The bridegroom took his new bride to a motel where they spent two days. On the morning of the third day he abandoned her and never saw her again.*
> *The bride was twelve years old. She was just a child—a child who got into a hasty and terrible marriage.*
> *Today I would like to inform you about a national problem in the United States—child marriages. This topic means a lot to me because when I was eleven years old, my parents and I moved from China to the United States. When I was twelve, I became that child bride I just told you about!"*

The above introduction did all the right things. It made the audience want to hear the rest of her speech. It was natural and interesting, and the audience understood why Maylin had chosen that topic for a speech.

In summary, start dynamically, make your purpose clear and begin the body of your speech. Refer to page 83 ("Preparing an Attention-Getting Introduction") in Chapter 5 for additional information about preparing the introduction to your speech.

Outlining

THE PURPOSE OF AN OUTLINE

An outline makes it easy for you to deliver your speech. It assures that you have organized your ideas and helps you remember all your information. With a good outline, you will never have to worry about forgetting what you want to say. Even when you are not giving a speech, an outline can make your life easier. You need never again forget something that you have to do. For example, let's say you have several errands to run after class. You could organize them as follows:

Outline of Errands to Run

I. Post Office

II. Grocery Store

III. Gas Station

IV. Bank

When one item doesn't depend on another, any random order of organization is fine. However, suppose your car's gas gauge reads empty and you don't have any money to pay for the gas. You would have to change your organizational pattern. Your new Outline of Errands would look like this:

Outline of Errands to Run

I. Bank

II. Gas Station

III. Post Office

IV. Grocery Store

O.K. You have a lot on your mind and could easily forget what you specifically want to do at each of the above places. No problem! Add the specific subpoints to each main item of your "Outline of Errands." For example:

I. Bank
   A. Cash check from Uncle Mario
   B. Deposit check from mother into savings account
   C. Pay $15.00 fine for bouncing a check
II. Gas Station
   A. Fill up tank
   B. Check water in battery
   C. Check oil level
   D. Put more air in left front tire

As you can now see, the key to outlining is to identify main topics and break them down into subtopics. With such an outline, you will never arrive home having forgotten something you had to do! Do this for your speeches and you will never again worry, "What if I forget what I was going to say?"

OUTLINING YOUR SPEECH

Now that you have gathered enough information to prepare the introduction, body, and conclusion of your speech, you are ready to reorganize and outline it.

A GOOD OUTLINE MEETS THREE BASIC REQUIREMENTS

1. Each idea must relate to and help prove the main point.
2. Each unit of the outline should contain only one idea.
3. Ideas should not be redundant or overlap each other.

1. Each Idea Must Relate To and Help Prove the Main Point.

EXAMPLE: I. Alcoholism is an International Problem.
   A. The Soviet Union has a high alcoholism rate.
   B. France has the highest alcoholism rate in Europe.
   C. Alcoholics have more car accidents than non-drinkers.
   D. Japan has a severe juvenile alcoholism problem.

QUESTION: Which supporting idea above does not belong? Why?

ANSWER: C does not belong. Although it is an interesting fact about alcoholics, it does not directly support I. Alcoholism is an International Problem.

2. Each Unit of the Outline Should Contain Only One Idea.

EXAMPLE: I. Small Cars Have Advantages Over Large Cars.
   A. They are less expensive and easier to park.
   B. Small cars get better gas mileage.

QUESTION: What is wrong with the above?

ANSWER: Point A contains two separate ideas. The information should be outlined as follows:

I. Small Cars Have Advantages Over Large Cars.
   A. They are less expensive.
   B. They are easier to park.
   C. Small cars get better gas mileage.

3. Ideas Should Not be Repeated or Overlap Each Other.

EXAMPLE:
I. Students Dislike the School Cafeteria.
A. There is very little to choose from.
B. The food is too expensive.
C. The menu is extremely limited.

QUESTION: What is wrong with the above?

ANSWER: Points A and C overlap each other. They express the same idea. Three separate non-overlapping points might be:

I. Students Dislike the School Cafeteria.
   A. There is very little to choose from.
   B. The food is too expensive.
   C. The silverware is always dirty.

REVIEW TEST

On the line to the left of each number, write the letter of the choice which best describes the outlined information:

a. *incorrect because each idea must relate to the main point*

b. *incorrect because each unit of the outline should contain only one idea*

c. *incorrect because ideas should not overlap each other*

d. *correctly outlined*

1. _____ I. Polyester Is Better Than Cotton.
   A. It is less expensive and easier to wash.
   B. It lasts longer.
   C. It requires less ironing.

2. _____ I. Madrid Has Many Fascinating Places.
   A. The Prado Museum houses wonderful art works.
   B. The Plaza del Sol is vibrant and exciting.
   C. Spain is famous for its sangría wine.

3. ____ I. Attending College Is Very Expensive.
   A. Tuition fees are quite high.
   B. It costs a fortune to go to college today.
   C. The costs of books rises every year.

4. ____ I. Juvenile Delinquency Is A Problem Nationwide.
   A. It's a problem in the Southern and Northern regions.
   B. It's a problem in the East.
   C. It's a problem in the West.

5. ____ I. Cats Make Wonderful Pets.
   A. They are easy to care for.
   B. They were worshipped in ancient Egypt.
   C. Cats provide excellent companionship.

6. ____ I. Reasons for Students' Parking Problems on Campus
   A. A large number of spaces are reserved for faculty.
   B. There are too many students with cars.
   C. Many outsiders illegally park in the lots.

7. ____ I. Abortion Should Be Illegal.
   A. It is the taking of a human life.
   B. Many doctors consider it to be murder.
   C. It is religiously immoral.

8. ____ I. Many Religious Groups Support the President.
   A. Jews support him.
   B. Catholics support him.
   C. Italians support him.

9. ____ I. Gambling Takes Many Forms.
   A. Casino gambling
   B. Horse racing
   C. Lotteries

10. ____ I. Ways to Fight Inflation
    A. Comparison-shop for best prices.
    B. The annual inflation rate is approximately five percent.
    C. Buy on sale.

CLASSROOM ACTIVITY

The following partial outline contains the complete title, introduction, and conclusion of a brief speech. Some of the main headings and supporting ideas have already been filled in. Using the pieces of information provided, complete the outline. The finished product should show a well-organized outline of a speech.

A FABULOUS FANTASIA CRUISE

Introduction

I. Are you wondering where you can go on your next vacation without going bankrupt? I have the perfect solution for all of you: Take a "Fantasia Cruise."

II. You will soon agree that it is affordable, the accommodations are great, and many exciting adventures and activities await you.

Body

I. Financial Considerations

    A. Two adults cruise for the price of one.

    B.

    C.

II.

    A. All cabins are fully air-conditioned.

    B.

    C.

III. Ship's Facilities

    A.

    B. Swinging disco open all night.

    C.

    D.

IV.

    A.

    B.

    C.

    D. Cozumel, Mexico

V. Shore Visit Activities _____

    A. _____

    B. Activities for sports lovers _____

        1. _____

            a. Waterskiiing _____

            b. _____

            c. _____

        2. Land sports _____

            a. _____

            b. _____

    C. _____

VI. _____

    A. Afternoon and evening bingo in captain's lounge. _____

    B. _____

    C. Competitive games _____

        1. _____

        2. _____

    D. _____

    E. _____

Conclusion

I. I think you will now agree that a "Fantasia Cruise" can be very affordable, and that you will enjoy luxurious accommodations and a wide range of unforgettable activities to keep you busy and happy.

II. Your dream vacation awaits you. Make your reservation soon and cruise to paradise with Fantasia!

The following informatiion is presented in random order. You must decide what to use and where to use it in the incomplete outline provided above.

Mid-week discounts are offered.	There is a color TV in each cabin.
Gambling casino open 24 hours a day	Children under 12 travel free.
Olympic-size swimming pool	Every cabin has a porthole.
Port-au-Prince, Haiti	Guided tours of each port visited
Guest Accommodations	Three elegant restaurants for your dining pleasure
Shipboard Activities	Visits to four exotic ports of call
Water sports	
Ping-pong tournaments	Nightly entertainment in ship's nightclub
Sailing	
Costume party	Puerto Plata, Dominican Republic
Poolside shuffleboard tournaments	Hiking
Georgetown, Grand Cayman	Passenger talent show
Shopping for native crafts	Horseback riding
	Fishing

FOR HOMEWORK

The following examples are word-for-word manuscripts poorly disguised as outlines. Re-do the information in correct outline form. Remember, a good outline meets the three basic requirements described on page 61.

EXAMPLE 1:   I. Since it lasts longer and costs less, polyester is better than silk; in addition, it is easier to care for.

     A. It may be washed twice as many times before wearing out and its color doesn't fade as quickly.

     B. Polyester doesn't have to be dry-cleaned and ironing is unnecessary.

EXAMPLE 2:   I. There are many things to do on a visit to Mexico including going shopping and visiting interesting places.

      A. You will enjoy visits to Chapultepec Castle, the Aztec Pyramids in Teotehuacan, and the Ballet Folklórico.

      B. You can shop for native crafts such as colorful embroidered blouses, hand-woven rugs, silver jewelry, and items of onyx including ashtrays, vases, and bookends.

EXAMPLE 3:   I. The United States exports products to countries in several continents. These include South America, Brazil, Argentina, and Asia.

      A. Other places receiving U.S. exports are Japan, China, and Colombia.

      B. In Europe, Spain, France, and Germany receive U.S. exports.

• *PRONUNCIATION TIPS*

English is one of the few languages in the world in which the "th" sound is consistently heard. Because it doesn't exist in most other languages, you might not be pronouncing it properly. A common error is to say the sound "d" instead of "th."

EXAMPLE: If you substitute "d" for "th": **they** will sound like **day**

those will sound like **doze**

> *Pronunciation Tip:* Pronounce "th" by placing your tongue between your teeth. Look in a mirror; make sure you can see the tip of your tongue as you say "th."

EXERCISE A: Read the following words aloud. (Look in a mirror if necessary!) Be sure you can *see* and *feel* the tip of your tongue protrude between your teeth.

they	o**th**er	ba**the**
then	mo**th**er	smoo**th**
that	fa**th**er	clo**the**
those	bro**th**er	soo**the**
there	ei**th**er	brea**the**

EXERCISE B: Clearly pronounce the following pairs of words aloud. Place your tongue *between* your teeth for "th" and *behind* your teeth for "d."

"**th**"	"**d**"
they	day
then	den
there	dare
breathe	breed
latter	ladder

EXERCISE C: Read the following phrases and sentences aloud. Remember to protroude your tongue *between* your teeth as you say the "th" sound in each of the boldface words.

1. **mother** and **father**.
   This is my **mother** and **father**.

2. **other brother**
   Will your **other brother** be **there**?

3. get **together**
   Let's get **together another** day.

4. **bathe the** baby
   Grandmother must **bathe the** baby.

5. **than the other**
   This is better **than the other** one.

5 Speaking To Inform

Look—a computer chip!
Everything you have ever learned
can be placed on one small chip.
Of course, our speech teacher's knowledge
would require *two chips!*

We live in a world of words and must be able to use the right words to make ourselves clear to people. In a few days you will be giving your first informative speech. You may worry that you will never be able to speak clearly enough to give a "real" speech. *Don't worry.* In this chapter you'll learn how to make interesting and effective informative speeches.

WHAT DO WE MEAN BY "INFORMATIVE SPEAKING"?

The major purpose of an informative speech is to give clear and correct information to listeners which will teach them about something. Your listeners should enjoy and be interested in the information you present. Informative speaking is all around us. Whenever you hear a report being made, a teacher giving an explanation, or a talk at a group meeting, you are hearing an informative speech. Please remember that the main purpose of speaking to inform is to present information to an audience so that they will understand and remember it.

WHEN DO WE MAKE INFORMATIVE SPEECHES?

We make informative speeches *all the time!* We might be asked to direct a stranger to his destination; we might need to explain to an auto mechanic exactly what is wrong with our car; or we might need to describe an illness to a doctor. Our goal in such informative talks is to state our ideas as simply and as clearly as possible.

CLASSROOM ACTIVITY

Now let's try an informal and fun information-sharing activity. Arrange your chairs in a large circle. Your teacher will call on you to choose one of the following questions to answer. Remain seated and relax as you share your information with the class.

1. Describe how birthdays are celebrated in your country.

2. Inform us about the educational system in your country.

3. Explain what are the national sports of your country.

4. Describe the climate in your country.

5. Inform the class about the geography of your country.

6. Describe the procedure for being admitted to this college.

7. Inform the class about your country's major cities.

8. Describe the procedure for registering for classes at this school.

9. Inform us about your country's important industries.

10. Explain how Christmas is celebrated in your country.

11. Describe the typical foods people eat in your country.

12. Inform us about a popular tourist attraction in your country.

13. Inform the class about the most important holidays in your country.

14. From the building you are now in, inform a "lost" student how to get to the:

   a. library
   b. gymnasium
   c. college bookstore
   d. cafeteria
   e. admissions office
   f. advisement or counseling department
   g. college auditorium
   h. international student department

Preparing for the Informative Speech

Preparing for Your Speech to Inform Will Include:

1. Analyzing Your Audience

2. Selecting Your Subject

3. Narrowing Your Subject

4. Gathering Information

5. Preparing Visual Aids

1. ANALYZING YOUR AUDIENCE

You should start preparing for your informative speech by looking at your future audience. Your job is to get as much information about your audience as you can. This information will help you prepare a speech which is relevant and interesting to your listeners. So—what do you need to know about your audience?

1. *Age:* What is the age range of your audience? If they are young, an appropriate speech topic might be "Choosing a Career." If they are middle-aged, a good topic might be "Planning for Retirement."

2. *Sex:* What is the sex distribution of your audience? If there are both males and females in your class, choose a speech topic that will be interesting to both men and women.

3. *Occupation:* Is your audience made up of college students who don't work? Or do most of your classmates have jobs? If they have jobs, where do they work? What do they do? If members of your audience have occupations in common, you could build your speech on this common background.

4. *Economic level:* What is the general financial position of your audience? You would not, for example, try to inform the average college student about "How To Build a Sauna in Your Jet Plane." However, it might be a great topic for a group of Texas oilmen or Arabian sheiks!

5. *General background:* It's also important to know something about your audience's general background, attitudes, and even religious beliefs. It would be inappropriate, for example, to talk to people who practice the Hindu religion about "The Best Steak Restaurants in Buenos Aires." People who are against smoking would not be interested in a speech about "Different Types of Cigarettes and Cigars."

FOR HOMEWORK

This speech class will be your audience for the rest of the semester. You should have already learned some important information about your classmates. Write a specific and complete analysis of your class "audience" which will help you in preparing your future speeches.

FOR CLASSROOM DISCUSSION

Discuss which of the following informative speech topics would be appropriate for presentation to an audience of

a. businessmen

b. high school students

c. working mothers

d. unemployed workers

e. single parents

f. college students

g. young professionals

Be sure to explain why each of the above "audiences" would or would not be interested in hearing the following speeches.

A Foolproof Diet	Ways to Fight Inflation
A European Vacation	Marriage Customs in Saudi Arabia
Home Decorating Hints	New Fall Fashions
Stamp Collecting	The Use of Computers in Business
Planning Your Career	Choosing a College
Coping With Divorce	Applying for a Part-time Job
Writing a Résumé	Hazards of Smoking
Investing for Retirement	Importance of a Good Education
Raising a New Baby	How to Tune Your Car's Engine
Taking an African Safari	The Ancient Aztec Civilization

2. SELECTING YOUR SUBJECT

Your first reaction might be "What shall I talk about?" This problem is not as big as you think it is. The truth is that there is a quick and easy way to select a topic for an informative speech. What is this "secret" that will help you? Just this: Pick a topic that you know a great deal about or that really interests you! Try to talk about something that you have had some experience with.

EXAMPLE 1: A student in our speech class made a speech to inform entitled "Problems Facing Immigrants in a New Country." This student came to the United States from Poland at the age of 18. He experienced a variety of problems adjusting to life in America and was able to make his informative speech about a topic he personally experienced.

> **EXAMPLE 2:** Another student made a terrific speech about "Emeralds." In Colombia, she had worked for her father, who bought and sold emeralds. She too had experience with and a strong interest in her topic.

> **EXAMPLE 3:** A third student made an excellent speech about "The History of the Postage Stamp." His favorite hobby was stamp collecting, which he started at the age of 9. For this reason, he was very knowledgeable and interested in his topic.

The informative speeches described above were particularly good because the students chose topics they were really interested in and that they already knew something about. So—think about your special interests, hobbies or personal experiences. You will have no trouble choosing a topic!

3. NARROWING YOUR SUBJECT

Now that you have a topic for your informative speech, you must narrow it down. If you picked a topic that you know a great deal about, you probably know more about your subject than the audience does. That is important, but—there is a danger in this. You might want to tell all you know about your subject. Trying to tell all you know about a particular subject in one speech would be a very bad idea, for two reasons:

First: Your teacher will probably give you a time limit of about five minutes for your speech. Let's say you were going to talk about your favorite subject, "Soccer." It would be impossible to say everything there is to say about soccer in five minutes. You would have to limit your topic. For example, you could limit your talk to "The History of Soccer," or "The Worldwide Popularity of Soccer," or "The World Cup Tournament," or "Basic Rules of Soccer."

Second: Your audience will not remember many details or much information after just one speech. You must limit your topic so that your audience will understand and remember it. For example: let's say you wanted to talk about Mexico City. If you tried to tell too much about Mexico City (its history, climate, geography, social and political problems, restaurants, museums, etc.) your audience would never remember it all! You could limit your topic to: "Mexico City's Fascinating History," or "Shopping in Mexico City," or "Popular Tourist Attractions in Mexico City."

There are three things to remember about limiting your topic:

I. A good informative speech topic should be *specific.*

II. A good informative speech topic should contain *one* idea.

III. A good informative speech topic should be *achievable.*

What Do We Mean by "The Topic Should Be Specific"?

We mean that you must *limit* your topic (as previously discussed) and know your specific purpose in giving your speech. Be sure to avoid topics that are too general. *Example:*

The topic "Hurricanes" is much too general.

The topic "Preparing for a Hurricane" is specific.

The topic "Causes of Hurricanes" is specific.

The topic "Dangerous Effects of Hurricanes" is specific.

What Do We Mean by "The Topic Should Contain One Idea"?

We mean that your speech should have just one purpose. Most audiences would be very confused if you made a speech that was about two different subjects. *Example:*

The topic "Choosing a Hotel and Buying a Car in a Foreign Country" contains more than one idea. It would not make a good speech.

The topic "Choosing a Hotel in a Foreign Country" contains *one* idea.

The topic "Buying a Car in a Foreign Country" contains *one* idea.

What Do We Mean by "The Topic Should Be Achievable"?

We mean that your audience must actually be able to do something or understand and remember specific information after your speech is over. If you try to speak about something very complicated and difficult to understand, your audience will feel completely lost after your speech is over. *Example:*

> The topic "How To Weave an Oriental Rug" is not achievable. Your audience would not be able to weave an Oriental rug after your speech.

> The topic "How to Buy an Oriental Rug" is attainable. Your audience would actually be able to use this information if they ever went shopping for an Oriental rug. They would remember what to look for.

> The topic "Building a Computer" is not attainable. The audience would probably not understand your information or be able to build a computer after your speech.

> The topic "The Use of Computers in Education" is attainable. Your audience could learn valuable and relevant information about the importance of computers.

FOR CLASSROOM DISCUSSION

Some of the topics listed below would not make for good informative speeches because they are either too general, contain more than one idea, or are not achievable. Some would make good topics. Discuss each of the following and decide which would make appropriate speech topics and which would not. Be sure to explain why you feel the way you do.

EXAMPLE A: "South America" (This topic is too general.)

EXAMPLE B: "How to Become a Concert Pianist" (This topic is not achievable.)

EXAMPLE C: "The Significance of Dreams" (This topic is specific and something the audience would understand and remember.)

Musical Instruments   Writing a Résumé

Buying a Used Car   Child Abuse

How to Fly An Airplane

Applying For a Bank Loan

Ecuador

Choosing and Caring For a Parrot

Basic Techniques of Dog Training

Life Saving Uses of Snake Venom

The History of the Hawaiian Islands and Alaska

The Best Way to Lose Weight

The Use of Marijuana in Medicine

The Galápagos Islands

Chinese New Year Traditions

Birds

Snakes

The Celebration of Three Kings Day in Mexico and Christmas in Germany

4. GATHERING INFORMATION

Now that you have selected and limited your topic, you need to gather information so you can prepare the actual speech. There are two places to look for material for your speech:

1. *Look within yourself for information.* Do you remember the example (p. 75) of our student from Poland who made his speech about "Problems Facing Immigrants in a New Country"? He first looked within himself for information about the topic. Write down what you already know about your subject.

2. *Look outside of yourself for information.* Looking outside of yourself means talking to other people who know something about your topic, and looking for books, magazines, or encyclopedias that have additional information.

Your goal should be to find more information about your subject than you can use! This will make you even more knowledgeable about your topic. You will then have a choice about what information to use and what to ignore. Your teacher will give you guidelines about looking outside of yourself. You might be required to consult a minimum of two printed sources (books, periodicals, magazines) for information and to turn in a completed copy of the "Outside Sources Consulted" form on the next page.

Student's Name _____ Date _____

Outside Sources Consulted

Title of Book or Periodical _____

Name of Author _____

Pages Read _____

Publisher and year _____

Title of Book or Periodical _____

Name of Author _____

Pages Read _____

Publisher and Date _____

(If you used a person as an additional outside source, provide the information requested below.)

Name of Person Consulted _____

Person's Occupation _____

Date of Interview _____

Describe why this person is qualified to provide information about your topic:

_____

_____

_____

_____

_____

_____

_____

5. PREPARING VISUAL AIDS

Pictures, charts, models, and diagrams help to make a speech clear and interesting. They help the audience to actually see and experience what you are talking about.

EXAMPLE 1: If you were making your speech to inform about "Funeral Customs In Japan," this picture of an actual Japanese hearse would make your speech more interesting.

EXAMPLE 2: If you were speaking about "Marriage Customs in Japan," this picture of a Japanese bride and groom in traditional dress would help your audience understand what you were describing.

We hope you will use visual aids when making your informative speeches. The following guidelines about using visual aids are important for you to know:

1. *Your visual aids must be large enough for everyone to see.*
2. *Do not pass out objects or papers during your speech.* If people are looking at objects or reading papers, they will not be listening to what you are saying.
3. *Keep charts, maps, and graphs very simple.* Don't try to show too many details in one visual aid.
4. *Look at your audience—not at your visual aids!* When you are showing a picture, graph, etc., be sure to maintain eye contact with your listeners.
5. *When you are finished using your visual aids, put them away.* If you were starting to speak about Retiro Park in Madrid, it wouldn't make sense to have your audience continue looking at a picture of a bullfight!

Organizing Your Informative Speech

> ## *Organizing Your Speech to Inform Will Include:*
>
> 1. Preparing an Attention-Getting Introduction
>
> 2. Preparing a Preview of What You Are Going to Talk About
>
> 3. Preparing the Main Body of Your Speech
>
> 4. Preparing a Summary of What You Spoke About
>
> 5. Preparing a Memorable Conclusion

1. PREPARING AN ATTENTION-GETTING INTRODUCTION

The opening of your speech is very important. You must have your audience's immediate attention and get them interested in your speech at the very beginning. You must make them want to listen to your speech. If this sounds like a difficult task, it is! But—it's not impossible! We will now teach you different ways to prepare an interesting, attention-getting introduction.

1. *Make your audience curious.* Ask your audience a question. They will immediately be interested in knowing the answer. For example, one of our students started her speech with this series of questions:

> *What can cost ten dollars or a thousand dollars?*
> *What can be every color of the rainbow?*
> *What can you wear on your arm, your cheek, your leg, or even your back?*
> *What do famous movie stars and authors have?*

Are you curious? We are sure that you would like to hear more of the speech. This student made her informative speech about "Tattoos."

2. *Begin your speech with a story.* People like to listen to a story. They want to find out what it is all about. For example, a boy from Colombia started his speech with this story:

> *A guard took me to a square room with no lights. The room was so black I couldn't even see my own feet. All of a sudden a hidden electric wall slid closed behind me. There was no way out. I thought I was in a tomb. All of a sudden bright lights came on. I was surrounded by gold on all four sides!*

Did this story make you interested in hearing this speech? Of course it did! This student made his speech about "The Gold Museum" in Bogotá, Colombia.

3. *Begin your speech with a well-known quotation.* One of our students began her speech about "The Disadvantages of Borrowing" with the famous quotation from *Hamlet* by William Shakespeare:

> *Neither a borrower nor a lender be, for loan oft loses both itself and friend.*

4. *Begin your speech with a startling or shocking fact.* Example:

> *You can get almost anything you want without cash! And you can begin today!*

This statement got your attention, didn't it? A student of ours used this striking statement to begin his speech "The Billion Dollar Business of Bartering." (He talked about ways to use your skills or services to get almost anything you want without cash.)

2. PREPARING A PREVIEW OF WHAT YOU ARE GOING TO TALK ABOUT

After your terrific attention-getting opener, you must provide your audience with a preview of what you are going to talk about. The best way to do this is to tell your listeners exactly what you are going to say.

> **EXAMPLE 1:** In a speech entitled "Surviving a Hurricane" you could use the following preview:
>
> My purpose today is to tell you what to do in the event of a hurricane. I will talk about:
>
> > A. How to prepare for a hurricane
> >
> > B. Safety measures to take during the hurricane
> >
> > and C. What to do after the storm is over

> **EXAMPLE 2:** In a speech about "Left-Handed People" you could use the following preview:
>
> In discussing left-handed people, I will:
>
> > A. Explain the causes
> >
> > B. Talk about problems that left-handed people have
> >
> > and C. Tell you about some world-famous "lefties"

3. PREPARING THE MAIN BODY OF YOUR SPEECH

Now that your listeners know exactly what you are going to talk about, it is time to present your information. Be sure to present the main parts of your speech just the way you said you would.

4. PREPARING A SUMMARY OF WHAT YOU SPOKE ABOUT

Although you have finished presenting all your information in the main body of your speech, you are not ready to sit down. Every good speech should have a summary of the information presented. The best way to summarize your information is to remind your audience about what you said. Help your listeners remember what you spoke about by repeating the main points covered in the main body of your speech.

EXAMPLE 1: In the speech about "Surviving a Hurricane" you could use the following summary:

Well, I've given you some very important information today. You now know:

A. How to prepare if a hurricane is coming

B. Various safety measures to take during the storm

C. What to do after the hurricane is over

EXAMPLE 2: In the speech about "The Olympics" you might use a summary like this:

As you can see, the Olympic Games are very important to people all over the world. I hope you learned some interesting information about:

A. The history of the Olympics

B. The Olympics today

C. The future of the Olympic Games

5. PREPARING A MEMORABLE CONCLUSION

You still aren't ready to sit down! You must do one more thing before your speech is finished. You must end your speech effectively. Never end your speech with "That's all I have to say. . . ." The final words of your speech are the ones your audience will remember. It's important to conclude with a statement that will leave your audience thinking about what you said. The techniques for concluding speeches are the same as those for beginning speeches. Refer back to "Preparing an Attention-Getting Introduction" on page 83. These suggestions will also help you when preparing your memorable concluding remarks.

EXAMPLE: In the speech about "Surviving a Hurricane," a memorable and effective conclusion could be the following:

For 12 hours in the black of night, it was like a nightmare. In the morning we saw crushed cars and roofless houses. But we survived, because we knew what to do!

LET'S REVIEW HOW A TYPICAL INFORMATIVE SPEECH SHOULD BE ORGANIZED

Introduction

Gets the audience's attention

Preview Statement

Tells the audience what you are going to talk about

Main Body of the Speech

Contains your main ideas presented in a logical order

Summary Statements

Helps your listeners remember what you spoke about

Memorable Conclusion

Ends your speech gracefully

SAMPLE OUTLINE

The following is a sample outline of an informative speech. You can see that this speech has all the important parts that have been described in this chapter.

Stage Fright

Attention-Getting Introduction

Can you guess what famous dancers, singers, actors, politicians, and executives have in common with us—students in a speech class? I'll tell you. It's called *stage fright*!

Preview of What You Are Going to Talk About

This is something we all have in common. Today we will be learning four major points about stage fright.

First: Some different symptoms of stage fright

Second: The causes of stage fright

Third: Famous people who have had stage fright

Fourth: What can be done about it

Transition to
Main Body:

> **Stage fright affects everyone differently.**

Main Body of Speech

I. Symptoms of stage fright
   A. Some people say their heart pounds faster than normal.
   B. Others tell how their hands begin to shake.
   C. Some people complain that they perspire a lot.
   D. Other people claim that their legs feel week.

Transition:

> **Although the symptoms of stage fright might vary for all of us, its causes are quite simple.**

II. Reasons for stage fright
   A. Many people worry that they'll forget what they want to say.
   B. Others are afraid that they'll look silly.
   C. Some people think the audience won't like them.
   D. International students might worry that their English isn't very good.

Transition:	**You'll be pleased to know that if you get stage fright, you're in very good company.**

III. Famous people have admitted to stage fright
    A. Winston Churchill once said that he thought there was a block of ice in his stomach each time he made a speech.
    B. Julio Iglesias has revealed in interviews that he is nervous about his pronunciation when speaking English.
    C. Carol Burnett, the famous comedienne, has admitted to having stage fright before facing an audience.

Transition:	**Although you might feel better knowing that even the rich and famous get stage fright, you're probably wondering what can be done about it.**

IV. What you can do about stage fright
    A. Be thoroughly prepared and practice many times before a presentation.
    B. Take your time before you start to speak.
        1. Take several deep breaths before beginning.
        2. Put your notes on the speaker's stand and establish eye contact with your audience before beginning.
    C. Remember that stage fright is normal.
    D. Remember that your listeners are your friends; they want you to do well.

Transition to Summary:	**I hope you learned some new things about stage fright today.**

Summary of What You Spoke About

You should now understand four major points about stage fright: its symptoms, its causes, famous people who have had it, and what you can do about it.

Memorable Conclusion

The next time you feel nervous about making a speech, just tell yourself "To heck with stage fright, I know my stuff and I'll do great!"

GRADED INFORMATIVE SPEECH PRESENTATION

Now that you know how to prepare (page 73) and organize (page 83) an informative speech, it's time to make a presentation in front of the class. Be sure to consult with your teacher during the preparation of your speech.

   Due Date: _____

   Time Limits: 3–5 minutes (Practice and time yourself.)

GUIDELINES

Choose any topic that:

1. Interests *you.*

2. *You* know something about.

3. You can limit to be SPECIFIC and ACHIEVABLE.

EVERY SPEECH MUST HAVE THE FOLLOWING:

Attention-Getting Opener: The first thing you say must get our attention and make us want to hear your speech.

Preview: After the opener, you must tell us exactly what you are going to speak about.

Main Body: This is where you describe and explain the information you know and researched. Organize your ideas into main points. Use visual aids when appropriate.

Summary: After you finish discussing your final main point, you must review with us all main points in your speech.

Memorable Conclusion: The last thing you say should provide a graceful finish to your speech. Never end abruptly or by saying, "That's all."

Use the following worksheet in the preparation of your speech. Refer to the sample outline for "Stage Fright" as necessary.

Informative Speech Preparation Worksheet

1. Decide on some possible topics that interest you. Write them here.

   _____

   _____

   _____

2. Explain how you would narrow or limit your topics.

   _____

   _____

   _____

Discuss the above with your teacher. Decide on one topic and get to work!

3. Divide your topic into two or three important points to discuss in the main body of your speech.

   Point 1: _____

   Point 2: _____

   Point 3: _____

   (If you are unsure about the main points you've decided to talk about, show the above to your teacher. She or he will help you make your final decision.)

4. Prepare your interesting attention-getting opener.

   _____

   _____

   _____

   _____

   _____

5. Prepare a preview of the main points you will talk about.

_____

_____

_____

_____

_____

_____

6. Prepare a summary of the main points in the body of your speech.

_____

_____

_____

_____

7. Prepare a memorable conclusion.

_____

_____

_____

_____

_____

We expect that you will change the information on your worksheet several times. That's natural! After you are really pleased with it, you are ready to prepare your working outline. Use the format on the next page as your guide.

(Speech Title)

Attention-Getting Opener:

Preview of What You Are Going to Say:

Main Body of Speech:

Point 1: _____
(Write your supporting information for Point 1 below)

Point 2: _____
(Write your supporting information for Point 2 below)

Point 3: _____
                (Write your supporting information for Point 3 below)

Summary of Main Points:

Memorable Conclusion:

● *PRONUNCIATION TIPS*

Confusing spelling patterns and the similarity between sounds probably cause you to have pronunciation problems with several English vowel sounds. Two vowels that students frequently confuse are "ē" (as in s**ee**) and "ĭ" (as in **i**t).

EXAMPLE: If you confuse these sounds: **it** will sound like **eat**

sheep will sound like **ship**

> *Pronunciation Tip:* Be sure to *smile* and feel tension in your lips as you pronounce "ē." ("ē" is a long sound: p r o l o n g it!) "ĭ" is a short, quick sound. Remember not to smile and tense your lips as you would for "ē."

EXERCISE A: Read the following pairs of words and sentences aloud or repeat them after your teacher. *Smile* and feel lip tension as you say the words in Column I and *relax* your mouth as you pronounce Column II words.

I ("ē")	II ("ĭ")
fe**e**t	f**i**t
sh**ee**p	sh**i**p
t**ea**m	T**i**m
When did he sl**ee**p?	When did he sl**i**p?
She will l**ea**ve.	She will l**i**ve.
Change the wh**ee**l.	Change the w**i**ll.

EXERCISE B: Read the following sentences aloud or repeat them after your teacher. Circle the boldface words pronounced with the long vowel "ē"; underline those with short vowel "ĭ."

1. Please **sit** in the **seat**.

2. He **did** a good **deed**.

3. **Tim** made the **team**.

4. Potato **chips** are **cheap**.

5. The shoes don't **fit** my **feet**.

EXERCISE C: Read the following dialogue silently. *Circle* all words pronounced with long vowel "ē" and *underline* all words with short vowel "ĭ." Now practice the dialogue aloud with a classmate.

JIM: Hi, Tina! Do you have a minute?

TINA: Yes, Jim. What is it?

JIM: My sister is in the city on business. We will eat dinner out tonight. Can you recommend a place to eat?

TINA: There is a fine seafood restaurant on Fifth Street. The fish is fresh and the shrimp is great. But it isn't cheap!

JIM: That's OK. It will be "feast today, famine tomorrow!" I'll have to eat "frijoles" the rest of the week!

6 Understanding and Using Common Expressions

Don't let idioms trip you up!

Every language has popular expressions which are considered to be part of normal, everyday speech. Although these expressions are used frequently in conversational English, they are unique because they are composed of words which don't always mean what you would expect. These common expressions are known as idioms. An idiom cannot be translated literally. Attempts to do so often lead to confusion and frustration. For example, "You're pulling my leg" means "you're kidding or not telling the truth." It doesn't really mean that you are holding my leg and pulling on it.

Although you learn English grammar and vocabulary, it is important to develop the ability to use these common expressions. A knowledge of idioms will help you improve your speech communication skills. A familiarity with these expressions will enable you to better understand your American friends and will help you to express yourself in a natural, informal manner. Unfortunately, dictionaries don't always explain the meanings of idioms.

This chapter has been created to teach you a variety of these expressions in a meaningful context. Try to use idioms in your everyday speech whenever possible. As you study this chapter, your teacher will explain, give examples, and answer your questions.

IDIOMS WITH NAMES OF BODY PARTS

1. pull one's leg   (to joke about something or exaggerate)

   "Don't *pull my leg*, tell me the truth!"

2. leg to stand on   (proof or support for an idea or decision)

   "Without a witness, you don't have a *leg to stand on*."

3. last leg   (the final part, the last phase)

   "Asia will be the *last leg* of my around-the-world trip."

4. foot the bill   (pay the costs or expenses)

   "My father is *footing the bill* for my education."

5. stand on one's own two feet   (to be independent or responsible for one's own life)

   "Now that you are 21, you should *stand on your own two feet*."

6. put one's foot down   (to take a firm stand, to enforce a command)

   "My father *put his foot down* and won't let me use the car."

7. put a foot in one's mouth   (to say something embarrassing)

"Think before you speak so you don't *put your foot in your mouth.*"

8. make one's mouth water   (to make hungry or stimulate the appetite)

"The smell of mom's cooking *makes my mouth water.*"

9. melts in your mouth   (tastes very good, delicious)

"Grandmother's apple pie *melts in your mouth.*"

10. see eye to eye   (to agree completely)

"We get along well because we usually *see eye to eye.*"

11. pull the wool over one's eyes   (to deceive or trick someone)

"My teacher didn't believe my excuse, I couldn't *pull the wool over her eyes.*"

12. butterflies in one's stomach   (to be very nervous)

"When I speak before large groups, I get *butterflies in my stomach.*"

13. over one's head   (to be unable to meet responsiblities or pay debts)

"Stella can't pay her bills, she's *over her head* in debt."

14. lose one's head   (to act irresponsibly or foolishly without thinking; to become very excited)

"After I got a small raise, I *lost my head* and bought an expensive car."

15. out of hand   (to be out of control)

"The poorly conducted meeting got *out of hand.*"

16. lend a hand   (to provide help or assistance)

"I'll *lend a hand* and help my friend fix his car."

17. heart's not in it   (not interested or enthusiastic)

"My *heart's not in* doing housework today."

18. by heart   (to know by memory)

"I know the 'Pledge of Allegiance' *by heart.*"

19. slap in the face   (a bad insult)

"John called me stupid; that's a real *slap in the face.*"

20. elbow room   (space to move around)

"I don't like small spaces, I like lots of *elbow room.*"

21. hold one's tongue   (to keep quiet)

"Please *hold your tongue*, I don't want to hear it."

22. wet behind the ears   (to have very little experience)

"He's not ready to be the boss, he's still *wet behind the ears.*"

23. all ears   (to listen carefully)

"Tell me what is bothering you, I'm *all ears.*"

24. cross one's fingers   (to wish for good luck or success)

"I'll *cross my fingers* that you'll win the race."

25. on the nose   (perfect with no mistake; at that exact time)

"Your answer to that question was right *on the nose.*"

REVIEW TEST I (IDIOMS WITH BODY PARTS)

On the line to the left of each number, write the letter of the choice which best shows the meaning of the idiom in italics.

_____ **1.** Jose doesn't *stand on his own two feet.*

    a. He prefers to sit on a chair.
    b. He broke a leg and can't stand up.
    c. He always asks others to help him.

_____ **2.** Chocolate *makes my mouth water.*

    a. It makes me want some.
    b. It makes me thirsty.
    c. It takes away my hunger.

_____ 3. This is getting *out of hand.*

      a. The bird in my hand flew away.
      b. I burned my hand on the stove.
      c. The situation is out of control.

_____ 4. That was a *slap in the face.*

      a. My friend hit me in the face.
      b. My boss said I am lazy.
      c. A tree branch hit me in the face.

_____ 5. Ali is *over his head.*

      a. He is swimming in the ocean.
      b. He is a very short person.
      c. He can't pay his bills.

_____ 6. Susanna is *wet behind the ears.*

      a. She forgot to dry her ears after a shower.
      b. She doesn't have much experience.
      c. She got wet in the rain.

_____ 7. Kim doesn't know when to *hold his tongue.*

      a. He always tells important secrets.
      b. He can't roll his tongue up.
      c. He always sticks his tongue out when he is angry.

_____ 8. They don't *see eye to eye.*

      a. They never look at each other.
      b. They always wear dark sunglasses.
      c. They don't agree with each other.

_____ 9. That car is on its *last leg.*

      a. It only has one tire.
      b. It needs a paint job.
      c. It is about to break down completely.

_____10. You got that right *on the nose.*

      a. The ball hit your nose and broke it.
      b. A fly landed on your nose.
      c. You did the assignment perfectly.

Match the idioms in the left-hand column with their meanings in the right-hand column.

1. butterflies in one's stomach   to feel very nervous

2. foot the bill   to deceive someone

3. by heart   to be uninterested

4. pull the wool over one's eyes   pay the costs

5. heart isn't in it   by memory

6. lose one's head   to help out

7. elbow room   take a firm stand

8. cross one's fingers   to act foolishly

9. lend a hand   wish for good luck

10. put one's foot down   space to move

IDIOMS WITH NAMES OF FOODS

1. as easy as apple pie   (very easy to do)

   "A child could do it; it's *as easy as apple pie.*"

2. a piece of cake   (very easy to do) [same as above]

   I'll fix your car in ten minutes, *it's a piece of cake!*"

3. spill the beans   (to tell a secret)

   "Pierre *spilled the beans* and told me about the surprise party."

4. sardines in a can   (very crowded)

   "In Tokyo, people pack into the metro like *sardines in a can.*"

5. cry over spilled milk   (to worry about something that has already happened)

   "You lost your ring last year, don't *cry over spilled milk.*"

6. cream of the crop   (the best there is)

   "This perfect diamond is really *the cream of the crop.*"

7. it's a lemon   (a product with many defects)

"This new car is a *lemon*; nothing works right."

8. fishy   (when something seems to be wrong; probably not the truth)

"There is something *fishy* about his story; I don't believe it."

9. cool as a cucumber   (has a lot of self-confidence; in perfect control of a situation)

"The president is as *cool as a cucumber* even under pressure."

10. hot potato   (a topic that causes controversy; a subject that people argue about)

"The subject of capital punishment is a *hot potato*."

REVIEW TEST III (IDIOMS WITH FOODS)

Underline the choice which correctly explains the meaning of the idiom on the left side of the page.

1. spill the beans
   a. turn over the can of beans
   b. tell the secret
   c. drop the beans on the floor

2. piece of cake
   a. a slice of chocolate layer cake
   b. a portion of dessert
   c. very simple

3. something's fishy
   a. there are fresh fish
   b. fish will be served for dinner
   c. something seems to be wrong

4. easy as apple pie
   a. apple pie is fun to bake
   b. very easy to do
   c. apple pie is easy to eat

5. cry over spilled milk
   a. complain about something in the past
   b. cry because a glass of milk spilled
   c. the baby dropped milk on the floor

6. hot potato
   a. a controversial topic
   b. a potato which is too hot to eat
   c. a potato that isn't cold

7. sardines in a can
   a. these are sold in grocery stores
   b. a very crowded situation
   c. sardines packed with oil in a can

8. cream of the crop
   a. cream of mushroom soup
   b. cream for coffee
   c. the very best quality

9. cool as a cucumber
   a. very self-assured
   b. a cucumber which isn't hot
   c. the way you feel after a cool swim

10. it's a lemon
    a. a small yellow fruit
    b. a sour fruit used for lemonade
    c. a defective product

IDIOMS WITH NAMES OF COLORS

1. green with envy   (very jealous or envious)

   "When I won the prize, all my friends were *green with envy*."

2. feel blue   (to feel sad or depressed)

   "He was *feeling blue* because his dog died."

3. scared yellow   (to be very afraid)

   "She saw a ghost and was *scared yellow*."

4. see red   (very angry or mad)

   "My father *saw red* when I broke his new radio."

5. rosy   (good; favorable; bright)

   "Ricardo just inherited a lot of money; his future looks *rosy*."

6. to be green   (without experience)

   "She needs more training, *she's still green*."

7. in the red   (financial losses are greater than profits, not making a profit)

   "The owner is working hard to get his business *out of the red*."

8. in the pink   (to be in good health)

   "My doctor told me I was *in the pink*."

9. out of the blue   (unexpectedly; seems to come from nowhere)

"I haven't heard from my uncle in 15 years. Yesterday, he called me *out of the blue*."

10. white lie   (a lie which is unimportant; small fib)

"The woman told a *white lie*. She said her hair was naturally blonde."

REVIEW TEST IV (IDIOMS WITH COLORS)

On the line to the right of each word, write the name of the color usually associated with it.

1. jealous   _____   6. promising   _____

2. afraid   _____   7. unexpectedly   _____

3. unhappy   _____   8. angry   _____

4. healthy   _____   9. inexperienced   _____

5. in debt   _____   10. harmless untruth   _____

MISCELLANEOUS COMMONLY HEARD IDIOMS

1. under the weather   (not feeling well)

"Randy won't go to the party, he's a bit *under the weather*."

2. throw in towel   (to give up)

"Don't *throw in the towel*, finish your education."

3. putting the cart before the horse   (to do things backwards; reverse the correct order of events)

"I *put the cart before the horse* and bought an airplane before I learned how to fly."

4. make tracks   (to move fast)

"Let's *make tracks* and stop wasting time."

5. put two and two together   (to reach a conclusion; figure things out)

"We *put two and two together* and realized why mother was angry."

6. get to the point   (be specific; explain yourself clearly)

"I'm very busy, please *get to the point.*"

7. beating around the bush   (speaking in vague generalities; not being specific)

"Stop *beating around the bush*, and get to the point."

8. runs in the family   (characteristic shared among members of a family)

"All my sisters are tall, height *runs in my family.*"

9. eat one's words   (to take back what one said)

"When I learned I was wrong, I had to *eat my words.*"

10. squared away   (things are in order, problems solved)

"I'm finally *squared away* now that all the papers have been sent."

11. pull some strings   (to use influence; to manipulate)

"You're the boss's son, please *pull some strings* and get me a job."

12. face the music   (accept the consequences; take the punishment)

"The criminal had to *face the music* in the courtroom."

REVIEW TEST V (MISCELLANEOUS IDIOMS)

Substitute one of the following idioms for the italicized words in each sentence. Be sure to use the correct grammatical form of each idiom.

put two and two together	runs in the family
putting the cart before the horse	pull some strings
under the weather	squared away
get to the point	to eat one's words
make tracks	threw in the towel
face the music	

EXAMPLE: I used my father's boat without permission; now I am ready to *be punished*. (*face the music*)

1. The police *solved the mystery* and caught the thief.
    (_____)

2. You don't have much time; *be specific* and explain yourself clearly.
    (_____)

3. Carl called me a bad card player. He had to *take back what he said* when I won all the games. (_____)

4. The teacher told the class to *work faster* and finish their lesson.
    (_____)

5. Helga was discouraged and *gave up*. She dropped out of school.
    (_____)

6. Bill caught the flu. He's *not feeling well*. (_____)

7. All the problems with my new car have finally been *taken care of*.
    (_____)

8. Blonde hair *is a common trait in my family*. My mother and three sisters are all blondes. (_____)

9. I'd like to be an actress. Do you know anyone who could *use their influence* and get me a part in a movie? (_____)

10. Elena planned a big party for Linda without knowing if Linda could come. Elena always *does things backwards*. (_____)

CLASSROOM ACTIVITY

Your teacher will call on different students in the class to complete the following sentences. When it's your turn, finish the sentence with a response that shows you understand the meaning of the idiomatic expression.

EXAMPLES: a. The meeting was *out of hand* because everyone was shouting and throwing papers.
b. Good looks and intelligence *run in my family*!
c. We don't always *see eye to eye* but we like each other and are very good friends.

1. I finally *put two and two together* and _____.

2. I *feel blue* today because _____.

3. My car is a *lemon* because _____.

4. _____ *like sardines in a can.*

5. He *threw in the towel* _____.

6. Sue finally *spilled the beans* by _____.

7. I don't think her *heart's in her work* because _____.

8. My friend was *green with envy* _____.

9. Maria *put the cart before the horse* and _____.

10. _____ *on the nose.*

11. It's time to *put your foot down* _____.

12. I get *butterflies in my stomach* when _____.

13. The students got *out of hand* when _____.

14. _____ *makes my mouth water.*

15. I'll try to *pull some strings* and _____.

16. My mother *saw red* when _____.

17. I tried to *pull the wool over her eyes* by _____.

18. Julio had to *eat his words* after _____.

19. Elena was *feeling under the weather* because _____.

20. _____ *is as easy as apple pie.*

21. That sounds *fishy* because _____.

22. Please *lend a hand* and _____.

23. It's time to *make tracks* because _____.

24. I told my son I'd *foot the bill* for _____.

25. _____ *by heart.*

26. He *put his foot in his mouth* when _____.

FOR HOMEWORK

Try to figure out the meanings of as many of the following sayings as possible. Ask anyone who is willing to help you. Come to class next time prepared to discuss these idioms.

1. A stitch in time saves nine.

2. An ounce of prevention is worth a pound of cure.

3. A watched pot never boils.

4. The grass is always greener on the other side.

5. When in Rome, do as the Romans do.

6. When the cat's away, the mice will play.

7. People in glass houses shouldn't throw stones.

8. A bird in the hand is worth two in the bush.

9. Don't put all your eggs in one basket.

10. Don't count your chickens before they hatch.

11. You should look before you leap.

12. A rolling stone gathers no moss.

13. All that glitters is not gold.

14. It's useless to close the barn door after the horse gets out.

15. Birds of a feather flock together.

16. Old houses mended, cost little less than new before they're ended.

17. You can't tell a book by its cover.

18. Cross each bridge as you come to it.

19. It's easier to catch flies with honey than vinegar.

20. Half a loaf is better than none.

21. Strike while the iron is hot.

22. Give him an inch and he'll take a mile.

23. That's like borrowing from Peter to pay Paul.

24. The pot is calling the kettle black.

25. Too many cooks spoil the broth.

GRADED SPEECH PRESENTATION I

Now that you are an expert on the meanings of all the idiomatic expressions, it's time to make a presentation in front of the class. Your teacher will grade you on this speech, but don't worry. You'll do fine!

Directions for Presentation

1. Choose one of the sayings on the previous page that you like.

2. Explain in your own words the general meaning of the expression.

3. Describe two examples that illustrate the saying. Use your imagination and make them up if necessary!

(Your teacher will tell you if you are allowed to use notes.)

SAMPLE PRESENTATION

Expression: "*When the cat's away, the mice will play.*"

I. This saying means that animals *or* people might not behave if no one is there to supervise.

II. (Example #1) I left my two dogs at home alone while I went to the store. When I returned, I saw they had chewed a hole in the carpet. This would not have happened if someone stayed home to watch them. (*When the cat's away, the mice will play!*)

III. (Example #2) The teacher was giving his class a test. He went out of the room for a few minutes. When he returned, everyone was talking and telling each other the answers. If he had stayed in the room, the students could not have cheated. (*When the cat's away, the mice will play!*)

GRADED SPEECH PRESENTATION II

Now let's gain some practice using our common expressions in the context of an actual speech.

Directions for Presentation

1. Choose one of the expressions presented in the chapter.

2. Deliver the introduction to a speech. Begin with an attention-getting opener and end after the first transition. (Review page 83 about preparing good speech introductions.)

3. Be sure to use the common expression you select in either your opening remarks *or* transition.

SAMPLE INTRODUCTION

Expression: "A Hot Potato"

EXAMPLE #1:   Opening Remarks

"Have you heard the joke about political parties in Latin America? Every country has three parties. One is in, one is out, and one is marching on the capital!"

Transition

"The topic of politics in Latin America is **a hot potato**. It's a topic that causes controversy, one that many people argue about. I would like to explain why political parties change so often in Latin America.

EXAMPLE #2:   Opening Remarks

"Crime in America is **a hot potato**. People always argue about solutions to the problem. Many blame the police; the police blame the courts; the judges blame the prison system."

Transition

"It's time we stopped blaming the police, courts, and prison system! We can all take action and deal with this "*hot potato*." I am going to convince all of you to join your neighborhood Crime Watch Program."

● *PRONUNCIATION TIPS*

Contractions are two words which are combined to form one. They are frequently used in spoken English and are grammatically correct.

> *Pronunciation Tip:* **When participating in a conversation, use contractions whenever possible. Otherwise, your speech will sound stiff and unnatural.**

EXERCISE A: On the line to the right of each two-word expression, write its appropriate contraction.

Example: it is   ___it's___

1. does not   _____
2. I am   _____
3. should not _____
4. will not   _____
5. he is   _____

6. I will   _____
7. can not _____
8. we have _____
9. you are _____
10. is not   _____

EXERCISE B: Write ten of your own sentences using Exercise A contractions. Practice saying them aloud.

1. _____
2. _____
3. _____
4. _____
5. _____
6. _____
7. _____
8. _____
9. _____
10. _____

EXERCISE C: Read the following pairs of sentences aloud. The first sentence is written in full form, the second with the contractions. Notice how smooth and natural the second sentence sounds compared to the choppy formal sound of the first one.

1. Omar *does not* know. Omar **doesn't** know.
2. I *do not* think she cares. I **don't** think she cares.
3. *You are* coming, *are you not?* **You're** coming, **aren't** you?
4. *She is* very tall. **She's** very tall.
5. Antonio *is not* a good cook. Antonio **isn't** a good cook.

7

Speaking to Persuade

I have one of the most poisonous snakes known to mankind in this box. I am going to persuade each of you to gently touch my pet "Klunkunda"

WHAT DO WE MEAN BY "PERSUASIVE SPEAKING"?

The major purpose of a persuasive speech is to get others to change their feelings, beliefs, or behavior. Your goal in making a persuasive speech is to convince your listeners to do what you want them to do or to change their opinion about something to agree with yours. We are all faced with persuasive speaking on a regular basis. Whenever a salesperson tries to convince you to buy a product, a political leader tries to get you to vote a certain way, or your teacher lectures about why a history class should be required, you are hearing a persuasive speech.

WHEN DO WE MAKE PERSUASIVE SPEECHES?

We make persuasive speeches *all the time*. We might ask a friend to lend us money, ask our teacher for a higher grade, try to convince our sister to lose some weight, or try to persuade our father to buy us a new car. Our goal in all such persuasive talks is to try to change or influence others.

CLASSROOM ACTIVITY

We will now try to practice our persuasive speaking skills in some possible real-life instances. Your teacher will ask for volunteers to "role-play" the following situations. You will need to make an informal persuasive speech in order to accomplish your purpose. Be sure to give as many reasons as possible in order to convince the other person to agree with you.

1. You want to go on an overnight camping trip with friends. Convince your parents to let you go.

2. Your little brother doesn't want to do his homework. Convince him to do it.

3. A friend of yours thinks watching TV is a waste of time. Convince him/her it isn't.

4. A classmate received an F on an assignment and thinks it is because the teacher doesn't like him. Convince him that that is not the reason.

5. You've had the same job for two years. Convince your boss to give you a promotion.

6. Your father wants you to get married. Convince him you are too young.

7. Your teacher thinks someone else wrote a composition for you. Convince her or him you wrote it yourself.

8. You are running for president of the senior class. Convince a group of students to vote for you.

9. You just had your car repaired and you think the bill is too high. Convince the manager of the shop to lower the bill.

10. Your friend smokes too many cigarettes. Convince him or her to cut down.

11. You bought a radio that you decided you didn't really need. When you tried to return it to the store, the owner didn't want to refund your money. Convince the store owner to give you your money back.

12. Your mother believes all unmarried girls should be chaperoned when they date. Convince her that this isn't necessary.

13. You prepared a dinner for an American friend who wouldn't try some of the foods you cooked. Convince your friend to taste what you made.

14. Your friend is too shy to ask a girl for a date. Convince him to call her up and invite her out.

15. Your parents don't want you to work while you are going to school. Persuade them to let you get a part-time job.

Preparing for the Persuasive Speech

There are several steps you will need to follow when preparing your "Speech to Persuade." These will include:

1. Determining your specific purpose

2. Deciding on possible topics

3. Analyzing your audience

4. Gathering information

5. Preparing visual aids

1. DETERMINING YOUR SPECIFIC PURPOSE

There are three common purposes of persuasion that we will discuss in this chapter. Of course, you already know that the general goal of persuasive speaking is to convince your listeners to change a belief, opinion, or behavior. However, when preparing a persuasive talk, you must narrow this down further and decide on one of the following specific persuasive purposes:

I. To Convince Listeners to Change Their Belief That a Stated "Fact" Is Actually True or False

If this is your specific purpose, your goal is to convince the audience that a reported fact is either true or not true, that something actually will happen or won't happen, that an event was represented correctly or incorrectly. For example, a speaker with this specific purpose might try to convince you to believe:

A. Mexico City is the largest city in the world.

B. The defendant committed the crime.

C. Capital punishment is a deterrent to crime.

D. There is life after death.

On the other hand, a speaker with the same specific purpose might try to convince you that the above "facts" are *not* true!

> **EXAMPLES:** A. Tokyo is the largest city in the world.
>
> B. The defendant is innocent.
>
> C. Capital punishment does not prevent crime.
>
> D. Life after death does not exist.

II. To Convince Listeners to Change Their Opinion About the Value of Something

If this is your specific purpose, your goal might be to convince the audience that something is good or bad, important or unimportant, fair or unfair, better or worse than something else, helpful or not helpful. For example, a speaker with this specific purpose might try to convince you to have the opinion:

   A. It's unfair for foreign students to pay higher tuition.

   B. Required courses in college are not important.

   C. Dogs make better pets than cats.

   D. A foreign language should be required of all high school students.

   E. New York is more interesting than San Francisco.

III. To Convince Listeners to Change a Behavior

If this is your specific purpose, your goal would be to convince your listeners to do something they are not doing or didn't intend to do or to stop some behavior they currently practice. For example, a speaker with this specific purpose might try to convince you to:

   A. Donate blood for the campus blood drive.

   B. Stop drinking caffeinated coffee.

   C. Watch TV for a maximum of one hour daily.

   D. Learn to scuba dive for a hobby.

REVIEW TEST

Read the following list of persuasive speech topics. Write the letter of the choice which best identifies the specific purpose of each topic on the line to the left of each number.

   A. *To convince listeners to believe that a stated fact is actually true or false*

   B. *To convince listeners to change their opinion about the value of something*

   C. *To convince the listeners to change a behavior*

_____ 1. Everyone Should Learn to Give Artificial Respiration

_____ 2. Airplane Travel in the U.S. Is the Safest Way to Travel

_____ 3. Soccer Is a More Exciting Sport Than Baseball

_____ 4. The Government Should Prohibit All Cigarette Advertising

_____ 5. Lower Highway Speed Limits Save Lives

_____ 6. Single Parents Should Be Allowed to Adopt Children

_____ 7. History Is a More Important Subject than Biology

_____ 8. Donate at Least $50.00 a Year to Your Favorite Charity

_____ 9. Alcoholic Beverages Should Not Be Sold on Sunday

_____10. Parrots Make Wonderful Pets

2. DECIDING ON POSSIBLE TOPICS

As with some of your previous speeches, your first worry is probably "What will I talk about?" Well, don't worry! We have several suggestions to help you decide on a few topics which would be appropriate to use for the actual persuasive speech you will present before the class.

As with your other speeches, it is important to select a topic that really interests you or that you have strong feelings about.

Start with yourself. Look for things that concern you as a person.

> **EXAMPLE 1:** One student's persuasive speech topic was: **"The Use of Seat Belts in Cars Should Be Required by Law."** This student had been in a serious car accident in Germany. He suffered only minor injuries because he was wearing a seat belt.

> **EXAMPLE 2:** An Oriental student who had a brown belt in karate made his persuasive speech on the topic **"Everyone Should Learn Karate as a Form of Self-Defense."**

The persuasive speeches described above were good because the speakers chose topics about which they had already formed firm opinions and beliefs. Think about your own attitudes and feelings. Be sure to choose a topic that you, too, feel strongly about.

There are two other things to consider when selecting your persuasive speech topic:

1. *People are more likely to change their beliefs, opinions or behavior if the change you suggest isn't too large.*

It is much easier to convince an audience to change their feelings or behavior a little bit than to persuade them to *completely* change their minds.

EXAMPLE 1: It would be very difficult to convince a heavy cigarette smoker to stop smoking completely. However, you might be able to persuade him or her to cut down to one pack a day.

EXAMPLE 2: It would be unrealistic to try to persuade a person of the Buddhist religion to become a follower of the Hindu religion. But—you might be able to convince him or her to read a book about Hindu customs.

EXAMPLE 3: It would be much easier to persuade someone who is afraid of heights to learn tennis than to persuade that person to try sky-diving as a hobby.

2. *Choose a topic that is arguable or controversial.*

Your topic should be one with which a large portion of the class has reservations or disagrees. Do not choose a topic that most people already agree with.

EXAMPLE 1: The topic "Exercise Is Good for You" is not a good topic. Most people already agree with this statement. However, "Jogging Is Healthier Than Swimming" or "Everyone Should Enroll in an Exercise Class" are topics that are arguable or controversial. Not all people agree with these claims, while most people already agree that "Exercise Is Good for You."

EXAMPLE 2: The topic "English Is Spoken All Over the World" is not controversial. Most people already know that. However, the topic "Everyone Should Learn English as a Second Language" or "English Should Be Required in South American Schools" are topics which could be argued. Many people might not agree with these opinions.

FOR HOMEWORK

For your next class meeting, be prepared to present at least three possible persuasive speech topics that you might like to use. Following are several general subject areas for you to consider. What are some of your personal views about these issues and subjects? If you have a strong opinion about any of the following, you may have just discovered a topic for your persuasive speech!

(You are not limited to the following suggested subject areas. They are merely presented as "food for thought." Try considering one of the many political, economic, educational, or social issues which are always in the local, state, national, or international news.)

Abortion	Separation of Church and State
Racial Equality	College Entrance Requirements
Prostitution	Legalization of Marijuana
Capital Punishment	Boycotting the Olympic Games
Arranged Marriages	Opportunities for the Handicapped
Nuclear Weapons	Smoking in Public Places

Gun Control	Living Together Before Marriage
Donating Money to Charity	The Legal Drinking Age
Working Mothers	Punishment for Dishonesty
Drunken Drivers	Mercy Killing
Animal Experimentation	Violence on Television
Pornography	Highway Speed Limits
Women's Rights	Required College Courses
Sex Education in Elementary School	Students Evaluating Teachers

My Three Possible Persuasive Speech Topics Are:

1. _____

2. _____

3. _____

3. ANALYZING YOUR AUDIENCE

We previously discussed audience analysis in Chapter 5: Speaking to Inform. Now it is important to explain audience analysis for the purpose of persuasive speaking. It will be necessary to learn as much as possible about your audience's feelings and opinions toward the topic you choose. You will need to know *how* they feel and *why* they feel that way in order to do a good job preparing your persuasive speech.

You can expect your listeners to feel one of three ways about the topic you choose for your persuasive speech:

1. They Might Agree Completely.

In this event, your audience already feels the same way you do. They already agree with your belief or point of view. (If this is the case, you must choose a *different* topic for your speech.)

2. They Might Be Indifferent.

In this event, your audience may have the attitude "*Who cares?*" (If this is the case, you must find out *why* they are indifferent or uninterested in your topic.) In your speech, you will need to convince them: (a) to be interested in the opinion you are presenting, (b) that it is important to consider, and (c) that they should adopt your opinion.

3. They Might Disagree Completely.

In this event, your audience simply does not agree with your point of view. They have the opposite opinion from yours or one which is completely different. They probably have definite reasons for feeling the way they do. If this is the case, you must find out their specific reasons for disagreeing with your opinion. In your speech, you will need to convince them that their specific reasons for disagreeing with the claim you are making are not good reasons.

CLASSROOM ACTIVITY

Now that you have several topics in mind for your persuasive speech, you are ready to analyze your audience. Your teacher will ask you to present your topics for group discussion to determine how your classmates feel about them. Use the following Survey of Opinions Form as a guide. Fill it out as your proposed topics are discussed.

SURVEY OF OPINIONS FORM

Persuasive Speech Topic: _____

General Audience Reaction to Opinion
(Circle One)

| Strongly Disagree | Disagree | Indifferent Uninterested | Agree | Strongly Agree |

If your classmates are indifferent, they are indifferent because: (circle the reasons)

1. They don't think your topic is important.

2. They don't feel your topic affects them.

3. They never heard of your topic.

4. They have never given your opinion any thought.

5. Other _____

If several of your classmates disagree with your opinion, you will find they probably disagree for different reasons. Ask them their specific reasons for disagreement. List below.

1. _____

2. _____

3. _____

4. _____

4. GATHERING INFORMATION

Gathering information for your persuasive speech will take a little work—but it is well worth your effort. Before you can organize your material, you must first collect it! A good way to begin is to write down what you already know about your topic. Remember, *start with yourself*. Think about your own observations or personal experiences which relate to the point you wish to make. Once you've done this, you're ready to gather additional information necessary for an effective presentation.

You are probably thinking, "How do I do this?" or "Where can I get the information I need?" There are several ways to obtain good evidence to use in your speech.

General Sources of Information: Ask the librarian to help you find material for your speech. He or she will probably provide more sources than you will need! There are many government publications which cover almost unlimited topics. The editorial pages in your local newspaper frequently discuss controversial subjects and provide excellent sources for you to quote in your speech.

The Readers' Guide to Periodical Literature: This guide lists the names of hundreds of topics and subjects and the different popular magazines which have articles written about those areas. For example: a student's persuasive speech topic was "There Is a Great Need for Strict Gun Control Laws in the United States." By looking up "gun control" in the *Readers' Guide to Periodical Literature*, he was directed to relevant articles in past issues of such magazines as *Newsweek*, *Time Magazine*, and *Ladies' Home Journal*. He used the information from these articles in his speech.

The New York Times Index: This index lists thousands of different subject areas. It will give you the date and page number of the issue of the *New York Times* newspaper which printed an article about your topic.

Personal Interviews: Talk to qualified people who have knowledge or opinions about your topic. Calling specialists on your subject and asking them questions might give you valuable material to use in your speech. Sometimes a personal interview with a specific person will be necessary. Call them in advance; explain what you would like to talk to them about, and schedule an appointment.

> **EXAMPLE 1:** A student's persuasive topic was **"The College Should Increase the School Library's Budget."** She called the head librarian, who felt the library needed additional books, more staff, and longer hours to better serve the students' needs.

EXAMPLE 2: Another student tried to convince the class that **"More Scholarships Should Be Available for International Students."** He interviewed the financial aid director at the university. The director agreed with him and provided specific information about the limited funds available to help international students with financial difficulty to continue their educations.

Whenever you use information from newspapers, magazines, or books, or quote specific people in your speech, be sure to tell your audience the source of your information. This will make your evidence and arguments more believable and impress your listeners. Hopefully, this will help you persuade them to agree with your persuasive claim.

As with the informative speech, your teacher might require you to consult a minimum of two outside sources (at least one should be printed; the other may be a person). Be prepared to turn in a completed copy of the Outside Sources Consulted Form on the next page.

Student's Name _____ Date _____

Outside Sources Consulted

Title of Newspaper or Magazine: _____

Name of Article: _____

Pages Consulted: _____

Date of Publication: _____

Title of Newspaper or Magazine: _____

Name of Article: _____

Pages Consulted: _____

Date of Publication: _____

Title of Book: _____

Author's Name: _____

Pages Consulted: _____

Publisher and Year: _____

(If you used a person as an outside source, provide the information requested below.)

Name of Person Consulted: _____

Person's Occupation: _____

Date of Interview: _____

Describe why this person is qualified to provide persuasive evidence supporting your claim:

_____

_____

What specific information used in your speech may be credited to this person?

_____

_____

5. PREPARING VISUAL AIDS

At times, the spoken word is not enough. Visual aids (pictures, graphs, or actual objects) can make your subject more interesting and be very powerful persuasive techniques. An audience is more likely to be convinced if they can actually "*see*" the importance or seriousness of the situation you are describing.

EXAMPLE 1: One student from France was trying to persuade us that "**France Has the Highest Alcoholism Rate in the World**." He said that one in ten of France's entire population suffers from alcoholism while in the United States, only one American in 30 has a drinking problem. He used the following graph to help the class "see" his statistics:

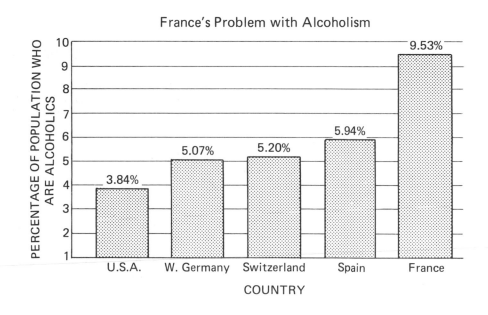

France's Problem with Alcoholism

EXAMPLE 2: In a speech to persuade students to complain to university officials about the polluted lakes on the campus, one of our students held up a large bottle of dirty brown water with a dead fish in it. He explained that the dead fish came from one of the nearby lakes. The students in the class were certainly convinced that this was a serious problem that should not be ignored.

EXAMPLE 3: If you were making a speech to persuade your classmates to donate money to a charity that helps handicapped people, this picture of handicapped children would probably cause them to react emotionally and want to make a donation to help.

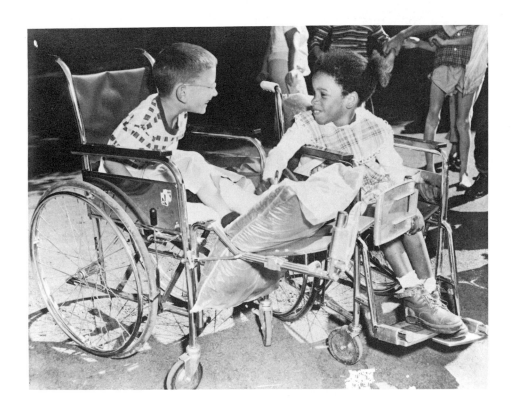

Organizing Your Persuasive Speech

Organizing your Speech to Persuade will include:

1. Preparing An Attention-Getting Opener

2. Preparing a Clear Statement of Your Specific Purpose

3. Preparing the Main Body of Your Speech

4. Preparing a Summary of Your Main Points

5. Preparing a Memorable Conclusion

1. PREPARING AN ATTENTION-GETTING OPENER

The introduction to a persuasive speech is very important. In order to convince listeners to agree with you, you must first make them trust you and see you as a person who thinks as they do. You must do this *before* you attempt to change their minds about something with which they currently disagree. The best way to do this is to begin your speech by talking about areas of agreement which are common to everyone. You can do this by first discussing:

A. *Common Goals.* (We all want the same basic things in life.)

B. *Common Problems.* (We all face this problem together; we are all concerned about this particular problem.)

C. *Common Experiences.* (We all know what it is like to . . .)

EXAMPLE 1: In a speech to convince people that "**Highway Speed Limits Are Too High**," you might begin: "Most of us know people who have had friends or family injured or killed in terrible car accidents on the highways. Certainly we've all read or heard about these tragedies in the news. We all want to live long, happy, healthy lives and not worry about the possibility of accidents. No one wants to worry whether he or she will arrive at their destination safely every time he or she gets in a car."

EXAMPLE 2: In a speech to convince us that "**Capital Punishment Should Be Legal**," you could first discuss the following common areas of agreement: "I'm sure everyone here is concerned about crime in our community. Many of us know that it isn't always safe to go out alone at night or even to walk through a dark parking lot to get to our car. All of us want to feel safe in our homes, cars, and on the streets. We would all like to see the amount of crime reduced."

EXAMPLE 3: In a speech to persuade the class to donate money to the International Red Cross, a student began with the following areas of agreement: "Although we take many things for granted, we all know how fortunate we are to have nice clothes to wear, a place to live, and plenty of food to eat. We all realize that many people in the world aren't so lucky. There are many starving and homeless people on every continent. Most of you would be willing to help people less fortunate than yourselves if you knew what to do."

2. PREPARING A CLEAR STATEMENT OF YOUR SPECIFIC PURPOSE

Now that you have discussed common areas of agreement and shown your audience that you are a sensible person with the same values and beliefs they hold, you are ready to clearly state your specific speech purpose. The audience should not have to guess what your persuasive purpose is, or wait until you are halfway through your speech to find out. *Now is the time to tell them!*

EXAMPLE 1: After building on areas of agreement about everyone's desire to avoid car accidents, etc. (Example 1, page 133), it would be effective to specifically state "There is a way to reduce the number of accidents and our concerns about highway driving: **The Maximum Speed Limit on U.S. Highways Should be 50 Miles Per Hour.**"

EXAMPLE 2: After discussing how lucky we all are to have good food, clothes, shelter, etc. (Example 3, page 134), it is time to state your specific persuasive purpose: "**Everyone in this Class Should Donate $5.00 to the International Red Cross**, which will use the money to buy food and clothing for needy people."

3. PREPARING THE MAIN BODY OF YOUR SPEECH

Now that your listeners know *exactly* what your specific persuasive purpose is, you must present support and evidence which will convince them to agree with you. This is where you must use the results of your Audience Analysis. At this point, some members of the audience will be indifferent to your topic or will disagree for specific reasons. Review your Survey of Opinions Form carefully before organizing this section of your speech.

I. Convincing Indifferent Listeners

People are indifferent about a topic because they do not see how it relates to them. In order to persuade listeners with the "*Who cares?*" attitude, you must get them interested in your topic. You must prove that your topic is important to think about, or that it directly affects them in some way.

EXAMPLE 1: Pretend that your persuasive purpose is to convince the audience to buy water purification systems for their homes. Listeners are likely to be uninterested in this topic because they never gave it any thought and don't believe it is important. However, you could tell them that the newspaper ran a story saying the quality of water in your community is the worst in the United States. Expert doctors warn that drinking this water could increase the risk of getting cancer. This type of information would certainly develop interest in your topic and get people to consider your suggestion.

EXAMPLE 2: After doing the audience analysis, one student found that several classmates were indifferent to her topic **"Casino Gambling Should Be Legal in Miami"** for the following reasons: Several students said it doesn't matter to them because they don't gamble; Some international students said they don't care because they will only live in Miami for a couple of years. The speaker showed them why they should be interested. She explained that casino gambling would help the city's finances and a proposed sales tax increase would not be necessary. She proved that everyone (gamblers and nongamblers; permanent residents and students on temporary visas) would benefit because prices in all stores and restaurants would be lower if the city sales tax was not increased. This type of evidence showed the indifferent students how this topic really does affect them.

II. Convincing Hostile Listeners

A "hostile" listener is one who completely disagrees with your opinion or belief. In order to persuade these listeners, you must know their reasons for disagreeing with you (your Audience Analysis gave you these), and convince them that their specific reasons for disagreeing are not valid.

EXAMPLE 1: Your specific persuasive purpose is to convince your classmates to donate blood to the blood bank of a local hospital. Your Audience Analysis shows that many people do not want to be blood donors. They are "hostile" or opposed for the following reasons:

A. One classmate is afraid to donate blood for fear of catching a disease from a dirty hypodermic needle.

You must convince him or her not to worry about this. In your "Gathering Information" step you called the hospital to get evidence to prove that this is not a valid excuse. Explain to the class that you interviewed the nurse in charge of the blood bank at the hospital. She explained that a different individually wrapped and sterilized needle is used for every blood donor. Needles are thrown away after each use and a new one used each time. Therefore, it is impossible to catch a disease from a dirty needle.

B. Another classmate doesn't have a car and thinks it is too much trouble to get to the hospital.

You must convince this person that this is not a good reason. In your "Gathering Information" step you learned it is very easy to get to the hospital and there are two choices: (1) There is a bus leaving from campus every fifteen minutes which goes directly to the hospital, and (2) If you call the hospital, they will send someone to drive you. This is free of charge to all blood donors.

EXAMPLE 2: Your specific persuasive purpose is to convince your listeners that "Capital Punishment Should Be Legal Throughout the United States." Your Audience Analysis shows that several of your classmates strongly disagree with this persuasive claim. They are "hostile" or opposed for the following reasons:

A. Capital punishment does not reduce crime.

You must try to prove this is not a good reason for disagreement. You could present evidence (based on your information-gathering research) that there are fewer murders committed in states that have the death penalty than in states that do not. You could also quote an expert in law enforcement who has stated that criminals are less likely to commit murder if they fear the death penalty.

B. Another classmate believes that murderers should not be put to death; they should be rehabilitated.

Again, you must convince this listener that his or her reason is not a good one. In your "Gathering Information" step you read about various rehabilitation programs for criminals that have been tried in different parts of the country. The results of studies designed to determine the effectiveness of attempts to rehabilitate criminals are not encouraging. You could report the results of specific studies which showed that the majority of law-breakers released from jail after participating in rehabilitation programs continue to commit the same crimes over and over.

C. Another classmate feels that life imprisonment is more humane than the death penalty.

You must present support showing why this isn't necessarily true. In your "Gathering Information" step, you learned that psychologists have surveyed hundreds of prisoners who are serving life sentences. The prisoners themselves said the thought of spending the rest of their lives in jail is unbearable; they wish they could have received the death penalty instead of a life sentence.

4. PREPARING A SUMMARY OF YOUR MAIN POINTS

Although you have finished presenting your persuasive support and evidence, you are not yet finished. An effective persuasive speech should summarize the support presented. You will do a better job of convincing people to agree with you if you briefly remind them why they should. Help your audience remember your information by repeating the main persuasive points you made in your speech.

> ***EXAMPLE 1:*** In the speech to convince others to become blood donors, you could summarize your main persuasive support like this:
>
> I'm sure you now realize that donating blood is:
>
>   A. Rewarding and worthwhile
>   a. Think of a dying person whose life you might save.
>   b. Think of the great personal satisfaction you'll have.
>
>   B. Perfectly safe and painless
>   a. Donating blood doesn't hurt a bit.
>   b. There is no chance of catching any kind of disease.
>
>   C. Very convenient
>   a. It will only take a few minutes of your time.
>   b. Free round-trip transportation to the hospital is available.

EXAMPLE 2: In the speech to convince that casino gambling should be legal in Miami, you could have a summary like this:

As you can now see, legalizing casino gambling in Miami would greatly benefit you and all residents of the city:

    A. A proposed sales tax increase will not be necessary

        a. This will keep prices you pay in restaurants lower.

        b. This will keep prices you pay in retail stores lower.

    B. Miami's finances will improve

        a. More money will be spent to improve the roads you use.

        b. More money will be spent to improve the public parks and beaches you enjoy.

        c. More money will be spent on educational materials for children in public schools.

5. PREPARING A MEMORABLE CONCLUSION

You are almost home free! You have just one more part of your speech to prepare: the conclusion. The conclusion of a persuasive speech should remind people to believe or do what you want them to. Try to make people think about the future and end with a short, direct reminder for them to take some type of action.

EXAMPLE 1: In the speech "**You Should Buy a Water Purification System for Your Home,**" a conclusion which makes people think about the future and reminds them to do what you want them to might be:

You might be healthy now, but think about your health in a few months or in several years. We all know that the water in this city can kill us! With a home purification system, you'll never worry about drinking polluted water again. For less than $20.00 turn your kitchen faucet into an ocean of fresh water. Buy a water purification system for your sink today!

EXAMPLE 2: In a speech to persuade people "**Everyone Should Enroll in an Exercise Class**," you could get people to visualize the future and remind them to take some kind of action with this conclusion:

Be the best you can be! Just think—in a few short weeks a beautiful, slender, athletic body can be yours. Heads will turn as you walk down the street. Be sure to make an appointment at your local health club right away!

LET'S REVIEW HOW A PERSUASIVE SPEECH SHOULD BE ORGANIZED

Introduction

Builds on Areas of Agreement Common to Everyone

Statement of Specific Purpose

Tells the Audience Your Specific Persuasive Claim

Main Body of the Speech

Contains Your Evidence to Convince People to Agree with You

Summary Statements

Reinforces Main Persuasive Points Presented in Your Speech

Memorable Conclusion

Reminds Listeners to Believe or Do What You Want Them To

SAMPLE PERSUASIVE SPEECH OUTLINE

The following is a sample outline of a persuasive speech. You can see that this speech has all the important parts that have been described in this chapter.

Make Your Next Vacation Chengde, China

Introduction Which Builds on Areas of Agreement

Have you ever wanted to go on vacation somewhere exciting but worried that it would cost too much? Or, haven't you ever worried that you might be bored once you got there? Of course, we all have! Everyone is nervous about these things before a vacation.

We all want the same thing from a vacation. We want adventure, excitement, great food, nice hotels, and we don't want to spend a lot of money!

Clear Statement of Specific Purpose

PLAN A TRIP TO CHENDGE, CHINA FOR YOUR NEXT VACATION

Transition to Main Body:

The magnificent city of Chendge will amaze and delight you. If you are worried that such a vacation will cost too much, you will be interested to know:

Main Body—Presentation of Evidence to Convince People

I. Chendge, China is very inexpensive
   A. The best hotel costs only $25.00 a night for a double room.
   B. You can eat three delicious meals a day for less than $5.00.

> **You might think that Chengde is ugly and you'll be bored there. Let me assure you this is not true.**

II. There are many things to see and do in Chengde
   A. See the most beautiful and unusual temples in the world.
      1. The Lamaist Temple of Universal Tranquility
         a. It was built by Emperor Qian Long in the 18th century.
         b. It has the largest wooden image of the Buddhist Goddess of Mercy, Guanyin.
      2. The Temple of Universal Joy was built in 1766.
         a. It has an incredible double terrace.
         b. See its fabulous double roof of yellow tiles.
      3. The Chinese Temple of Universal Love was built in 1713.
   B. Walk in and photograph the most beautiful gardens in China.
   C. Rent a rowboat and ride on one of Chengde's magnificent lakes.
   D. You can always go on a shopping spree.
      1. Visit one of the unique shops or department stores.
      2. Chengde is famous for several products.
         a. silk
         b. furs
         c. wood carvings
         d. hand-made Oriental rugs

Transition:

> **Some people fear getting ill and not finding a doctor if they travel to a small city in China. This should not be a concern.**

III. Medical care in China is excellent
   A. Chinese hospitals and doctors provide excellent care.
   B. There are many local clinics in all cities.
   C. Standard antibiotics and medications are available.

Summary of Main Persuasive Points

I hope I've convinced you to make your next vacation Chengde, China. Remember:

A. Chengde is a very inexpensive place to visit.

B. You'll never get bored because there is so much to see and do.

C. In the unlikely event you need it, excellent medical care is available.

Memorable Conclusion

You can stand on the same spot where China's most powerful emperors have stood. Your eyes will see the same green mountains they saw. You will be amazed by the spectacular scenery, cool breezes, and striking sounds. You will find your trip was worth the time and money you spent to get there. So, see your travel agent and make plans to visit Chengde, China soon!

GRADED PERSUASIVE SPEECH PRESENTATION

Due Date:
Time Limit: 3–5 minutes (Practice and time yourself.)
GUIDELINES

Choose a Persuasive Topic that:

1. You feel strongly about.

2. You truly want others to believe.

3. Is arguable or controversial.

Every speech must have the following:

Introduction: The first thing to do is to make us trust you and view you as a person who has the same basic beliefs and values we do. Begin by discussing common areas of agreement.

Clear, Specific Purpose: After building on common ground, tell us **exactly** what you want us to believe or do.

Main Body: This is where you present the support and evidence you gathered to prove your topic is relevant and important and to convince those who disagree with you to change their minds. Use visual aids when appropriate.

Summary: After presenting your final piece of persuasive support, you must review with us all the main points in your speech.

Memorable Conclusion: Your final remarks should make people think about the future and remind them to believe in your persuasive claim or take some type of action.

Use the following worksheet in the preparation of your speech.

Persuasive Speech Preparation Worksheet

1. Decide on some possible arguable or controversial topics that you feel strongly about. Write them below.

   _____

   _____

   _____

2. Determine your specific speech purpose for each of the above topics. (Refer to p. 120 as necessary.) Explain below.

   _____

   _____

   _____

   _____

   _____

3. Clearly state what your specific persuasive claim for each of the above topics would be in your actual speech. (Refer to p. 134 as necessary.)

   _____

   _____

   _____

Discuss the above with your teacher. Choose one persuasive claim and start gathering information.

4. List the most common reasons people have for disagreeing with or being indifferent toward your topic.

   Disagreement 1: _____

   Disagreement 2: _____

   Disagreement 3: _____

5. Prepare an introduction which discusses areas of agreement.

   _____

   _____

   _____

   _____

6. Clearly state your specific persuasive claim.

_____

7. Describe possible visual aids you could use to better convince your audience to agree with your claim.

_____

_____

_____

_____

The purpose of the above worksheet is to start you thinking about the kind of information you will need and how you will gather and organize material for your persuasive speech. After consulting a few different information sources, you will be ready to prepare your working outline. Use the following format to guide you.

_____

(Speech Title)

Introduction That Builds on Common Ground:

Specific Persuasive Claim:

Main Body of Speech:

Persuasive
Support 1: _____
(Write your support to convince indifferent listeners that your
topic is relevant and affects them)

Persuasive
Support 2: _____
(Write your support to answer or refute *Disagreement 1*)

Persuasive
Support 3: _____
(Write your support to refute *Disagreement 2*)

Persuasive
Support 4: _____
(Write your support to refute *Disagreement 3*)

Summary of Persuasive Points:

Memorable Conclusion:

The Persuasive Speech is an important presentation which will be evaluated and graded. The following are some aspects your teacher will consider.

I. *Delivery*
   A. Eye Contact
   B. Volume of Voice
   C. Rate of Speech

II. *The Speech*
   A. Adherence to Time Limits
   B. Introduction (Did you build on common areas of agreement?)
   C. Clear Statement of Specific Purpose
   D. Organization of Ideas
   E. Sufficient Persuasive Support
   F. Summary of Main Points
   G. Memorable Conclusion

III. *Other*

   Your teacher will also consider your use of visual aids (if any), your confidence and enthusiasm, and the overall quality and quantity of your research.

● *PRONUNCIATION TIPS*

The "Pronunciation Tips" at the end of Chapter 4 gave you an opportunity to practice the "th" sound in certain words and phrases. You were reminded not to substitute the sound "d" by mistake. However, in many other "th" words you might make the common error of saying the "s" or "t" sound instead of "th."

EXAMPLE: If you substitute "s" for "th": **thank** will sound like **sank**
              If you substitute "t" for "th": **three** will sound like **tree**

> *Pronunciation Tip:* Pronounce "th" by placing your tongue between your teeth. Look in a mirror; make sure you can see your tongue tip as you say "th."

EXERCISE A: Read the following words aloud. Look in a mirror and be sure to *see* and *feel* the tip of your tongue protrude between your teeth.

thing	heal**thy**	too**th**
think	weal**thy**	bo**th**
thought	some**th**ing	ear**th**
through	ba**th**tub	fai**th**
Thursday	bir**th**day	brea**th**

EXERCISE B: Clearly pronounce the following pairs of words aloud. Be sure to place your tongue *between* your teeth as you say the "th" words.

"**th**"	"**s**"	"**th**"	"**t**"
thumb	sum	three	tree
think	sink	thought	taught
thigh	sigh	thigh	tie
bath	bass	through	true
faith	face	both	boat

EXERCISE C: Read the following phrases and sentences aloud. Remember to place your tongue *between* your teeth as you say the "th" sound in each boldface word.

1. **thirty-third**
   Thelma had her **thirty-third birthday**.

2. **Thanksgiving**
   Thanksgiving falls on **Thursday**.

3. **through thick** and **thin**
   We remained friends **through thick** and **thin**.

4. **something** for **nothing**
   Don't **think** you can get **something** for **nothing**.

5. **author's theme**
   The **author's theme** is **thought** provoking.

8 Miscellaneous Speech Communication Activities

"Now I'm capable of anything!"

By now this speech class has been in progress for many weeks. No doubt you've already made quite a few speeches to your classmates. You have developed your self-confidence and the ability to speak before a group. This chapter contains suggestions for various miscellaneous speech communication activities. It presents guidelines for conducting a problem-solving group discussion, an intercultural/interpersonal communication interchange, a debate, a speech of introduction, and a "pick it up from here" speech.

Your teacher might assign or ask you to participate in one or more of the activities described in this chapter.

Problem-Solving Group Discussion

This is one of the most common types of small informal discussion groups. It consists of a small group of individuals seated around a table. The group members share their information and ideas in an informal and spontaneous manner. Their main goal is to get together in order to discuss a common problem and find solutions to it.

GUIDELINES

Due Date for Discussion: _____

Time Limit: 20–25 minutes

Number of Members Per Group: 4–5 (including group leader)

After the groups are formed, two very important things must be done before you can begin gathering information to use in the actual in-class discussion: You must choose a problem which is of interest and concern to all group members, and you must select a group leader.

CHOOSING A PROBLEM TO DISCUSS

Select a problem in which all group participants are interested. The discussion will be much livelier and more active if all group members feel personally involved and committed to the group topic. Consider problems which currently affect you as students or as residents of your community, city, etc. You might also consider problems which might not affect you now but could at some future point in time.

Suggested Problems for Group Discussion

Unfair Teachers	Campus Crime
Students Who Cheat	Child Abuse
High School Drop-outs	Juvenile Delinquency
International Terrorism	Airplane Hijackings
Alcoholism	Student Parking on Campus
Drug Abuse	Highway Automobile Accidents
Divorce Rate	World Hunger
Inflation	Drunk Driving
Teenage Suicide	Dirty Public Beaches
Rising College Costs	Apathetic Voters

Responsibilities of the Group Leader

The group leader has several responsibilities. In addition to participating with the other members in the discussion, he or she must:

a. introduce the participants

b. briefly state the problem to be discussed

c. take responsibility for starting the discussion

d. encourage all group members to participate in the discussion

e. make sure the organizational pattern is being followed

f. bring the discussion to a close after 20 or 25 minutes

ORGANIZATIONAL PATTERN

Before conducting the group discussion in front of the class, each member will have to gather information on the problem. In order to make sense and accomplish your problem-solving purpose, your information *must* be organized. All group discussions should follow the format outlined below.

I. Prove a Problem Exists
You must present evidence that your problem truly exists. Find statistics, refer to your own experience, interview authorities, give examples of specific incidences of the problem.

II. Explain the Causes of the Problem

You must present information that reveals the causes of the problem and explains why or how this problem developed.

III. Explain Future Effects of the Problem If Left Unsolved

You must predict what is likely to happen if the problem is not solved. Explain why it is important to solve this problem and show how people or society in general will be affected if this problem is allowed to continue.

IV. Present Possible Solutions to the Problem

Discuss the ways this problem might be solved. Present suggestions made by authorities and/or concerned or involved individuals. Give your personal opinions about how to solve the problem. Discuss the advantages and disadvantages of the proposed solutions.

All members are to inform themselves about the entire topic and all are responsible for the forward movement of the discussion. Everyone should feel free to comment, ask questions, and share information without being prompted by the group leader. Remember, in order to follow all the steps of the organizational format logically and thoroughly, *all* participants must be prepared and alert throughout the entire discussion.

Your instructor will advise you as to how this group discussion will be graded. You may be graded individually or receive a group grade for your efforts. In either case the following criteria will be considered:

I. Responsibility of Each Individual

    A. Evidence of Preparation

    B. Sufficient Number of Contributions

    C. Value and Constructiveness of Contributions

    D. Ability to Interact in Group Situation

II. Group Dynamics

    A. Group members felt free to express their opinions.

    B. The group stayed on the subject.

    C. All members participated.

    D. The group leader was helpful.

    E. No one person dominated the discussion.

    F. The leader introduced the problem clearly.

III. Organization

    A. The existence of a problem was proven.

    B. The causes of the problem were explained.

    C. The future effects of the unsolved problems were predicted.

    D. Possible solutions to the problem were presented.

E. There was agreement on the solutions to the problem.

Happy problem-solving!

Intercultural/Interpersonal Exercise

We all have beliefs (some correct, others incorrect) about other cultures and customs. The following informal classroom activity is designed to help you better understand and appreciate the different personalities of people from various cultures.

GUIDELINES:

I. Select a coin from your country that best represents **you** as a person.

   A. Bring the coin you chose to class.

   B. It should not be worth more than $1.00 in American money.

II. You should have good reasons for choosing your coin. They might be any of the following:

   A. The value of the coin

   B. The size or shape of the coin

   C. The color of the coin

   D. The inscriptions or picture on the coin

   E. The significance of the coin

   F. Various personal reasons

III. On the day of the activity, the class will be sitting in a large circle. You will be asked to:

   A. Explain your reasons for selecting your particular coin.

   B. Write the name of one of your classmates who you feel is the most worthy of receiving the coin.

   C. Give your coin to the person whose name is on your paper. You will do this *without speaking*, one student at a time, until all students have given away their original coin.

IV. Be prepared to answer these questions:

A. How did you feel if you received coins?

B. How did you feel if you didn't receive any coins?

C. Why do you think you received or didn't receive coins?

D. Can you think of any "real-life" situations that are like this exercise?

E. What have you learned about other cultures from this exercise?

Debating

A debate is a speaking situation in which opposite points of view are presented and argued. Each of the speakers participating attempts to influence the audience and convince them to agree with his or her ideas or beliefs. Basically, a debate as described in this chapter consists of two opposing speeches to persuade. A debate is an educational game; we know that you will find debating interesting and enjoyable!

RULES OF THE GAME:

There wil be two speakers in each debate: an *affirmative* speaker, and a *negative* speaker. The affirmative side always speaks in favor of the topic or proposition being debated; the negative side always disagrees with and speaks against the proposition. Each speaker takes turns speaking. When both are finished, the audience will decide which side won the debate.

The debate will consist of two distinct parts: the main speeches and the rebuttal. In the main speeches, debaters present their evidence and information to convince people to agree with them. In the rebuttal, the debater concentrates on attacking the opponent's position and tries to prove that his or her evidence should not be believed. Your debates will be organized as follows:

Affirmative speaker: 4 minutes
Negative speaker: 8 minutes
Affirmative speaker's rebuttal: 4 minutes

This format is fair as it gives each debater an equal opportunity.

CHOOSING A TOPIC TO DEBATE

Because both teams will be involved, pairs of opponents must consult each other and agree on the subject to be debated. You must form a proposition and decide who will speak in favor of it and who will argue against it. Refer to "Deciding on Possible Topics" (p. 122) in Chapter 7: Speaking to Persuade. These guidelines and suggested subject areas on page 124 will prove very helpful in your effort to select an appropriate debate topic.

Additional Suggested Debate Topics

Highway Speed Laws Should Be Lowered

Hitchhiking Should Be Legal

Students Caught Cheating Should Be Expelled From School

Professors Should Not Have Reserved Parking Spaces

Capital Punishment Should Be Abolished Worldwide

The Government Should Impose Rent Controls on Landlords

Students Should Drive Cars, Not Motorcycles

Interracial Marriages Should Be Illegal

The Use of Cocaine Should Not Be Legalized

Sex Education Should Be Taught in Elementary School

Required Courses in College Should Be Abolished

Prostitution Is Not Immoral

International Students' Tuition Fees Are Too High

PREPARING THE DEBATE

As previously mentioned, a debate is really two opposing speeches to persuade. Your main purpose is to convince your listeners that your ideas are correct and that they should agree with your point of view. Reread Chapter 7: Speaking to Persuade, to review information about making persuasive speeches.

ORGANIZING THE DEBATE SPEECH

The following is an outline of part of a sample debate. Remember, the affirmative speaker always agrees with the proposition, the negative speaker always disagrees with it.

PROPOSITION: Used Car Salesmen Are Dishonest

Affirmative Speaker (4 minutes)

I. Introduces the proposition and clearly defines or explains it.
  A. Defines his or her meaning of "used car salesman"
  B. Defines his or her meaning of "dishonest"

II. Establishes the problem: Most used car salesmen will cheat you if they can.
  A. Personal Example: My friend lost $500 when he sold his car last year. The salesman told him it was worth $1,000 on a trade-in. He could have sold it himself for $1,500.
  B. A used car salesman didn't tell my friend that the dealership wouldn't service the car after he bought it. (This was explained in the contract in very fine print that no one can see.)
  C. A used car salesman never mentions that the car you want has a history of mechanical problems.

III. Summarizes the affirmative view: In summary, most used car salesmen are dishonest.
  A. People lose hundreds or thousands of dollars when they buy or sell cars through used car dealerships.
  B. Used car salesmen are known to tell lies to convince you to buy an old car.

Negative Speaker (8 minutes)

I. Summarizes his or her disagreement with the affirmative speaker's information.

A. Accepts or rejects the other speaker's explanation or definition of the proposition.

B. Disagrees with the opponent's arguments: I disagree completely (and so should you) with what my opponent just presented:

1. that used car salesmen want you to lose money

2. that used car salesmen tell you lies

II. Disagrees with the proposition: Used car salesmen do not purposely try to cheat people.

A. I admit some people lose money, but it is their own fault, not the salesman's. A car dealer is in business to make a profit. They will pay you a fair price for your car. If you think it is worth more, you should try to sell it on your own.

B. A used car salesman doesn't force anyone to sign a contract without reading it. The affirmative speaker's friend should not have signed anything without reading it. If he had looked at it more closely, he would have known the dealership wouldn't service the car.

C. There is no rule that a salesman must volunteer information about a car's problems.

1. A salesman may use "omission." He doesn't have to supply information if you don't ask for it. It's the buyer's responsibility to ask specific questions about possible problems.

2. A buyer must do his or her homework and not rely on a salesperson to supply all the information. A buyer who doesn't do this is like an ostrich with his head buried in the sand!

III. Summarizes the negative view: In summary, used car salesmen are as honest as any group of sales professionals.

A. A salesman is in business to make as much money as he can.

B. A businessman would be crazy to say "That's too much profit for me, you should pay less money"!

C. People must think and argue for themselves. It's our own responsibility to learn to get the best deal we can when we buy or sell a used car. If we don't, it is our own fault.

Affirmative Speaker's Rebuttal (4 minutes)

The affirmative speaker now has one more opportunity to reemphasize his or her own ideas and destroy the negative speaker's information. The affirmative speaker should now:

A. Look at his or her first speech *point by point.*

B. Reiterate each point made.

C. Briefly restate how the negative speaker tried to attack it.

D. Reemphasize the point and give *more* evidence to reestablish it.

E. Briefly summarize and remind the audience to agree with the affirmative side of the issue.

Example of Affirmative Speaker's Rebuttal

I. The facts I presented in my opening speech still hold! I stated that:
   A. Most used car salesman are dishonest.
   B. They will cheat you if they can.
   C. They will tell lies to convince you to buy an old car.

II. The negative speaker tried, but could *not* prove me wrong!
   A. The negative speaker gave no evidence or examples to prove used car salesmen do not purposely cheat people.
   B. The negative speaker claims it was my friend's responsibility to read the fine print in the contract.
      a. If the contract was honest, it would be easy to read.
      b. If the contract was honest, it would be in large print.
   C. The negative speaker claims a salesman may use omission.
      a. A deliberate "omission" is a lie!
      b. One can't know everything about every car.

III. I know of two other people in this school who have been cheated by used car salesmen.
   A. Example 1: Humberto's Experience
   B. Example 2: Ulrich's Experience

IV. In summary, the negative speaker did not prove me wrong.
   A. Used car salesmen are dishonest.
   B. Please vote for the affirmative side of the proposition.

Speech of Introduction

A speech of introduction is one in which a person introduces a speaker to an audience. This type of speech has several important purposes: to acquaint the audience with the guest speaker, to help make the speaker comfortable, to interest the audience in the speaker and his/her subject, to announce the subject, and to give the speaker's name.

Your assignment is to introduce a "speaker" to your classmates. You will need to use your imagination and pretend that he or she is actually going to make a speech to the class. Your speaker may be some other person or one of your own classmates. Once you choose the person to introduce, you will need to decide for yourself the topic of your speaker's imaginary speech.

Suggested Speakers to Introduce

A Movie Star	An Expert on any Subject
A Famous Scientist	An Explorer
A Political Leader	An Artist
An Inventor	A Classmate
A War Hero	

A good introduction shouldn't be long—preferably two minutes or less. You owe it to the person you are introducing to be enthusiastic and to make your introduction sparkle. The best way to do this is to use the "T.I.S." formula.

"T" IS FOR TOPIC

1. Announce the subject the speaker will discuss.

2. Tell your audience the title of the speech. (Get this in advance from the person you are introducing.)

"I" IS FOR IMPORTANCE

1. Tell your audience why this topic is important to them.

2. Explain why this group of listeners will be particularly interested in the topic.

"S" IS FOR SPEAKER

Give the audience information which explains why the speaker is qualified to talk about this topic. Relevant background information might include information about the speaker's:

1. education

2. special training

3. travel experience

4. special honors

5. membership in clubs

6. professional experience

7. any other related achievements

The final words of your introduction should be the speaker's name. Be sure to pronounce the person's name correctly and to say it clearly and distinctly!

SAMPLE SPEECH OF INTRODUCTION

The following contains sections from a student's speech of introduction. Observe how well she used the T.I.S. formula!

"Topic"

Our speaker today is going to talk about "Why Small Businesses Fail."

"Importance"

Since this audience is composed mainly of business majors, you will find our speaker's information quite valuable. As many of you are planning to open your own business after graduation, or help run the family business, it is very important to learn how to prevent this problem from happening. You should be most eager to hear what our guest has to say.

"Speaker"

Our speaker today has studied business law and administration in Venezuela. He has a degree in business administration from the University of Caracas and graduated from there with honors. He is currently majoring in accounting at our university and is the president of the accounting society on campus. Our speaker helped supervise his father's import/export company for five years. As you can see, he is most qualified to speak on the topic. It is with great pleasure that I now introduce to you, *Mr. Carlos Alvarez.*

"Pick It Up From Here" Speech

The "pick it up from here" speech is a fun and informal classroom speaking activity which encourages you to think on your feet and use your imagination. One of your classmates will start a speech and talk for about one minute on any topic. He or she will then call on a classmate to continue the "speech" and talk for another minute. That student will call on one last person to speak for a final minute and conclude the speech.

GUIDELINES:

Due Date for Activity: _____

Time Limit: 1 minute per speaker.

Number of Speakers: 3 per topic

1st Speaker: a. Determines the topic or subject

b. Begins the speech and speaks for the first minute

2nd Speaker: a. Continues from where first speaker left off

b. Speaks for the second minute

3rd Speaker: a. Continues from where second speaker left off

b. Speaks for the third minute and concludes the speech

Your assignment is to prepare the first minute of a speech on any topic. Be prepared with this speech opener on the date set by your teacher. You might consider beginning your "pick it up from here" speech with a one-minute introduction about:

A Personal Experience   An Exciting Activity

A Pet Peeve   Particularly Annoying People

An Opinion about an Issue   A Family Argument

An Unpleasant Happening   An Incident That Angered You

SAMPLE "PICK IT UP FROM HERE" SPEECH

The following contains sections from a sample "pick it up from here" speech.

First Speaker

My best friend called one Saturday to ask if I would like to do two really fun things. First, take a drive in his new sports car, and second, go boating at the end of our drive. I said "Sure!"

It was a beautiful sunny day and we were driving with the sun roof open. The sun was shining and a cool breeze was blowing. We talked about how great the sailing would be when we got his sailboat out on the ocean. Then, without warning, something happened . . .

Second Speaker

What happened was that a highway patrol policeman stopped the car my friend and I were driving. The patrol car pulled alongside of us and pointed to the side of the road. We did not know what we did wrong because we were driving at the legal speed limit. After we were pulled over on the side of the road, the trooper told us that the trailer with the boat had no tail light. The trooper then became suspicious of us—probably because my friend was Colombian. He searched our car and boat and found two burlap bags in the back of the car. The trooper asked us what the bags contained and we told him that . . .

Third Speaker

The two burlap bags contained Colombian coffee. My friend had just arrived two days before from a visit to Bogotá, Colombia. His father owned a large coffee exporting company in the country. The policeman didn't believe us. He took us to the state police station. They took our coffee away from us and said it had to be tested. Finally, after realizing that we did nothing wrong, they gave us back the coffee and let us go.

We never did go sailing that day, but we did learn a new lesson about living in America. Never, never carry your coffee in a burlap bag that says "Colombian" on the side!

• PRONUNCIATION TIPS

Intonation refers to the use of melody and the rise and fall of the voice when speaking. It can determine grammatical meaning as well as the speaker's attitude. Correct use of intonation is necessary to convey your message correctly and to help you sound like a native English speaker.

Pronunciation Tips:

a. The pitch of your voice should **fall** (↘) at the end of declarative statements or questions that require more than a yes/no response (**who, what, when, why, where, which, how** questions). Examples:

I like school↘ She is kind↘ Where is it↘ Why should I do it↘

b. The pitch of your voice should **rise** (↗) at the end of statements expressing doubt or questions that ask for a yes/no response (*can, do, will, is* questions). Examples:

I think so↗ You ate 25 hot dogs↗ Will he stay↗ Did it rain↗

EXERCISE A: Read each of the following statements twice, first using a falling pitch and then a rising one. (Notice how the falling pitch helps you sound sure of yourself while the rising pitch causes you to sound doubtful or uncertain.)

Stated With Certainty↘	Stated With Doubt↗
You ran 55 miles.	You ran 55 miles.
He drank 8 gallons of wine.	He drank 8 gallons of wine.
She lifted 500 pounds.	She lifted 500 pounds.
They have 20 children.	They have 20 children.

EXERCISE B: Read the yes/no questions and sample answers aloud. Be sure your voice rises ↗ at the end of each question and falls ↘ at the end of each response.

Yes/No Questions↗	Responses↘
Can you see?	Yes, I can.
Are we leaving?	No, we're staying.
May I help you?	Yes, please do.
Is Sue your sister?	No, she's my friend.
Did he arrive?	Yes, he 's here now.

EXERCISE C: Read the following statements/questions aloud. On the line to the right of each sentence, draw the correct intonation arrow. ($\searrow$ = voice falls; $\nearrow$ = voice rises)

EXAMPLE: Can you sing?   _____$\nearrow$_____ (yes/no question)

1. I feel fine.   _____

2. When's your birthday?   _____

3. Did you see my friend?   _____

4. Why did Tom leave?   _____

5. We like to travel.   _____

That's all! Believe it or not, you have finished the last activity in the book. But this is really the beginning. YES, we said "The Beginning." Contrary to what you might think, this is *not* the end, but the beginning. It is now time for you to begin using the skills you have developed throughout this course. Remember Daniel Webster's famous words,

"If all my possessions were taken from me with one exception, I would choose to keep the power of speaking, for by it, I would soon regain all the rest."

We wish you the best of luck always.

Paulette Dale

James C. Wolf